Three-Handed Economist:

Interior Solutions in an Ideologically Cornered World

Written By:
Mark Flowers

MSP

Modern Sense Publishing
Conyers, GA 30094

I dedicate this work to my son, Gabriel, and my daughter, Abigail. Gabriel has taught me how to be patient, and Abigail has shown me the value of persistence. I hope they enter a better world as adults, than I live in now.

In Memory:
I'd also like to pay tribute to my close friend, Edgar "T.O." Ter-Oganessian, who is pictured as Atlas on the front cover. His tough love attitude and charismatic approach to life was always inspiring. T.O.'s life had meaning to all he encountered and everyone was his best friend. We miss you and can never repay the impact you had on our lives, except to try to live as you did. May you rest in peace until we all meet you once again.

What he taught me: Live well, say yes, take part, break bread, make time, be eager, be charitable, endure, and dream.

"It's not only what you eat, it's who you eat it with and the conversation is a side dish." – Edgar "T.O." Ter-Oganessian

Contents

Special Thanks

I'd like to submit my special thanks to William Manhire, without whom this book would never have been completed. His help has kept me driven, on task, and on point. Bill's edits and suggestions have been invaluable throughout the process of writing this book. I hope to have many works with Bill in the future, though one day I may have to bid him goodbye forever.

Thank you also to my wife, Cristine Flowers. She has been patient and understanding even when I've been difficult. I'm sure it has frustrated her on more than one occasion to find me sitting at my desk when she arrives home, and certainly when I continued writing after her arrival.

Thank you to my brother, Scott Flowers, who has been very encouraging, and to my mother and father.

Thank you to my colleague, Deborah Byrd. She made many suggestions and proofread the entire work.

Thank you to my children. When my son asks to play or my daughter demands attention, they have been very patient and loving even when I have not been as attentive as I had preferred or they would have liked. If it weren't for them, I would never have written this book. If it weren't for them, I would not have had a reason to write. If it were not for their amazing understanding, I would not have been able to complete this work.

Thank you to anyone else I may have forgotten, I appreciate what everyone has done to help with this endeavor.

Three-Handed Economist:

Interior Solutions in an Ideologically Cornered World

Part 1: Institutions and Politics

Chapter 1: History and Regulation

*"When we look at the world rationally, the world looks
rationally back."*

– Georg Wilhelm Friedrich Hegel

Introduction

President John F. Kennedy once said, *"Let us not seek the
Republican answer or the Democratic answer, but the right
answer."* This book seeks not *the right answer*, but the right
answer under the right conditions. It is not desirable to entrench
one's self into particular ideologies, philosophies, or restrictive
political framework. The hope is that we can successfully
employ a variety of solutions to an array of political and
economic problems. *Three-handed Economist* will present the
necessity of certain institutions and the benefits of newly
available provisions for health and welfare under improved
modern levels of wealth. Most importantly, it will discuss an
unorthodox solution for finally ending abject world poverty.

Economic philosophies have meandered through the entire
landscape of human thought for hundreds of years. People have
sought ways to better themselves, the lives of others, and to
produce goods more efficiently. From Karl Marx to Adam
Smith and modern day economists, hypotheses and theories have
inspired great thinkers to present their ideas and leaders to enact
their will. Ideas born from the minds of great people have grown
from mundane thought and inspired ingenious solutions.
Economic theories have evolved from simple barter and
exchange to complex monetary and fiscal interventions that are
inundated with important details, tradeoffs, and as yet
undiscovered consequences. Yet even with the immense number

of various philosophies, we still reduce economics to three basic models, building walls around our own particular philosophy and faulting those who disagree. After feudalism, free market models ruled nations for centuries, leading to increasing wealth gaps (the wealth difference between rich and poor) that often deepened levels of poverty. Poor economic conditions motivated peasants to demand more socialized solutions and gave birth to socialism. The Great Depression changed the way every government, even the laissez-faire regimes, viewed the unfettered markets and their role in the economy changed accordingly. Mixed approaches began swaying the political landscape.

Pure, free market economics requires an unbridled trust in the incentives produced by capitalist activities. One must accept that every action of every market participant will be in their own best interest, as well as the interests of society since goods and services will automatically flow toward their highest valued use. Through market-led economic structures, all the needed information will disseminate through the system, and with perfect efficiency it will lead to accurate pricing and better rationing of goods and services. As people become wealthier, incentives drive them to find ways to improve themselves with the creation of new inventions and employment of new innovations. Entrepreneurs will emerge to search for their own riches, investing in improved productivity and employing those who were previously unemployed as they rise to their ivory heights. Capitalists argue that markets can effectively push wages and prices to their sustainable, fair, and livable equilibrium state; the business cycle will be averted as the market automatically adjusts after-shocks and distortions, and a long-run state of level growth will be achieved. The claim of the free market capitalist is that there is no need for interventions into market activities; the market will self-regulate toward the most desirable outcome for everyone. As weaknesses emerge, markets will rise to void the imperfection. So on one hand, the capitalist hand, if governments would get out of the way of market activities, natural corrections would correct distortions and push economies back toward full employment, stable prices, and long-run economic growth.

Weaknesses in market-based solutions led to the creation of socialism. Socialist thought led some to believe that market structures were not sufficient to end the plight of so many who were suffering from low wages and capitalist-led worker abuses. Karl Marx, who gave a voice to socialist leanings and ultimately inspired its extreme form, communism, believed that government-directed economies would be the only way to reduce the income gap between rich and poor and an equitable distribution of goods and services could be reached. With the assumption that average workers would be sufficiently motivated with the knowledge that they were bettering everyone equally through their efforts, Marx argued that government should control or regulate all aspects of production, thus ensuring an equal share to every citizen. Workers should unite, take over ownership of industry and farming, and redistribute wealth from rich to poor. Through increased equity in wealth, better outcomes could be attained. The greatest weakness of free market capitalism, Marx believed, is best stated by Hernando DeSoto who wrote, "*The great contradiction of the capitalist system is that it creates its own demise because it cannot avoid concentrating capital in a few hands.*" If the government was in control of the means of all production, then equitably and efficiently distributing the wealth of society could be easily accomplished without the need for free market activity to direct prices and employment; the emergence of magnates could be mitigated, and the gathering of obscene levels of riches to any one person or family could be avoided. On the socialist hand, the claim is that governments would employ the working aged population and easily direct production levels to full employment, prices would be stable via government planned pricing, and growth would only require choosing proper investments as needs became evident.

There are any number of gradations between capitalism and Marxism, but here they will be consolidated under the simple heading of mixed-market economies. Ignoring the possibility of Market-Socialism, John Maynard Keynes argued that the business cycle was not a natural event that the free market could mitigate on its own. In fact it was well known that until the Panic of 1907 the business cycle had been increasing in frequency and in severity [1]. Since the free market had not functioned to slow or reduce the depth of the recessions or the peaks of accompanying growth, it was thought that government intervention in the markets might be necessary. In 1929 the stock market crashed, the markets failed to self-correct giving rise to ever-increasing levels of poverty among industrialized nations, and interventionist fiscal policy was born. Keynes argued that it was not governments who created the business cycle but the whims of market participants – what he referred to as the *animal spirits*. When aggregate demand is below normal, like during a recession, expansionary fiscal policy was prescribed. Conversely, when aggregate demand is higher than normal, such as during an economic expansionary period, the order of the day would be contractionary[1] fiscal policy. On the Keynesian hand, the argument is that government should spend during downturns to boost demand and contract spending during

---

[1] Contractionary fiscal policy refers to measures of a government to reduce spending and increase taxes. Sometimes this is done to balance a budget, or to reduce a national deficit and debt.

upturns to steer the economy back toward full employment, stable prices, and long-term growth.

There is no singular economic policy that is good under all conditions – that is the theme of this book. Free markets sometimes function efficiently and are very effective under the right circumstances. When free markets fail to address certain failures then fiscal directives might become necessary. When capitalism leads to worker abuses or other violations of citizens' implied rights then even extreme interventionist policies can be justifiably prescribed.

An unbridled, slow reacting, unregulated, market-driven economy has its merits and will always direct civilization toward a preferable outcome, if it is given enough time. For thousands of years humanity has existed with one form of market or another, and there is no reason to seriously consider that the unregulated, market-driven economy would not work again. When cycles emerge and corrections are needed there is no doubt the market will find the right solution eventually, but sometimes it takes too long to address potentially irreparable consequences in the process. The purely free market is easily exploited and rarely provides the protections it promises will eventually emerge, at least not in a timely fashion.

The purely Keynesian interventionist policy was designed to slow or eliminate the business cycle through counter-cyclical policies. Proponents of Keynesian interventionism hope to control the uncontrollable animal spirits through the use of fiscal policy. Often, however, interventionists exacerbate the peaks and valleys of the business cycle they hope to mitigate. Politicians have to debate policies, enact laws, and wait to see the effects of those policies, and that takes time. Unfortunately the timing must be perfect and information must be accurate for fiscal policies to effectively direct the economy back toward long-run, full employment levels. Without intervention the markets may adjust naturally, and there may have been no need for the fiscal policy Congress enacted, thus creating further distortions. Other times the information lag between the downturn and congressional action is too long and action occurs too late to mitigate the downturn or to slow a swift, and potentially harmful, upturn; thus the policy action is impotent. Furthermore, there may be political resistance to slowing a quickly growing, perceivably strong economy or even to boosting a weak or slow growing nation. Countercyclical policy requires expansion in bad times and contraction in good times, the political will to adopt sometimes unpopular policies, and the data to correctly predict where we are and where we are going. The tools of fiscal economic policy – changing tax rates or spending levels – are powerful, but political will to raise taxes or reduce spending in expansionary phases of the business cycle is often absent. Political influence ignores an important aspect of fiscal interventions; politicians are usually willing to adopt expansionary government policy but not the contractionary measures necessary to prepare for the next crisis.

Marx's ideology promised a central plan that would provide for a utopian world, organize the impossibly large and complex marketplace, and ultimately, on its own, it proved fatal to most of the economies it parented. With the exception of China – which suffered during its purely Communist era and is only now improving under more market orientated social policies – no socialist economy has ever proven successful in the long-term. Perhaps the problem lies in incentives as so many claim, or maybe it lies in the seclusionist[2] nature of socialist regimes and nations. One thing is certain: growth during communist regimes is usually slow, invention and innovation are easily stifled by government claims over ownership, and investment is difficult when property rights are not formally defined or politically protected.

That does not mean each system does not also have its own set of virtues. The free market has certainly created the right incentives to grow business and create jobs. New inventions improve production and increase our standard of living. Innovative new uses for capital have improved efficiency and helped the economy grow faster and more powerful. Keynesian fiscal policies helped stabilize the business cycle throughout the Great Depression, gave rise to huge science and technology programs initiated by the federal government during most of the Cold War, and most recently helped keep the world from another depression when fiscal policy was coupled with monetary policy. The inflationary nature of fiscal policy makes existing debt cheaper in the future, and pressures wages to increase over time in order to meet new levels of inflation. The bubbles that are sometimes created will eventually burst, but they give rise to growth and investment that may not have occurred otherwise. Some sustainable investments occur, as well as some unstable or frivolous ones, but overall we see a net gain in the long term. While those bubbles may not be real economic growth, they can motivate real growth. As markets self-correct and adapt to new economic conditions as they arise, and as bubbles grow and burst throughout the business cycle, opportunities are created and the population benefits. Bubbles create "disruptive" conditions that

---

[2] Seclusionist nature refers to the attitude particular nations sometimes take toward the rest of the world. To be seclusionist, a nation may retreat from world markets and sometimes even take more extreme measures such as closing their borders to trade, travel, etc.

are favorable to the introduction of good and bad inventions and innovations and allow the market an opportunity to direct resources to their highest valued use. There are also benefits to socialist mechanisms in an economy. The state can utilize fiscal policy to invest in roads, national defense, research and development, and more growth-promoting activities the free market may have ignored. When these systems are deemed desirable by society and adopted under a primarily market-driven economy, mixed-market economies emerge.

The state also has an obligation to address market failures. It is important to regulate certain industries the markets have failed to properly regulate, for example, when citizens or the environment are being exploited or irreversibly damaged. The negative externalities (costs borne by someone other than the market participant – things like air pollution, chemical dumping, etc.) produced by some industries can only be addressed by governments, since market mechanisms might ignore the problems for so long that a tipping point can finally be reached. Irreparable damage might be done and long-term economic impacts, impacts that could not have been anticipated or priced into the markets, might be realized. Government regulation is the only mechanism for stopping such actions.

The country must encourage or create incentives, sometimes through spending, to grow economies of scale and encourage investment into important technologies and industries that are simply too expensive for the free market to address. Only the government can protect private property rights, civil rights, public health, and the environment. Only the government can afford to invest in highways, sea-ports, national defense, universal education, and wide-reaching research initiatives and universities. Where private markets fail, governments fill the void.

Governments can, unfortunately, also violate citizens' rights and destroy their economies through their actions. There are countless examples of such problems around the world and even inside the United States during eras of oppression over certain groups or activities. Certainly government action can adopt counter-productive policies that increase unemployment, decrease investment, and cause outrageous levels of inflation. Government action is not free; all programs must be funded from tax dollars, industries must pay to comply with new regulations, and higher prices sometimes emerge in the markets due to increased compliance costs. Governments that misunderstand monetary policy or citizens who also ignore its implications can, for example, demand more money be distributed within the economy, giving rise to ludicrous amounts of inflation and ultimately doing more harm than good. When governments fail, they fail spectacularly. When the free market fails, it usually fails with a whimper.

Under the right conditions there would not be a need for regulation or government action. The central point of this book is that there is a forum for all ideas, an environment where every solution proves correct, and an environment where every solution proves incorrect. Finding that solution after identifying the conditions surrounding particular economies is what Jeffrey Sachs refers to as a *"differential diagnosis,"* comparing economic prescriptions to that of doctors and pharmaceuticals. Enlightened thought, vigorous discussion, and, ultimately, an opened mind will leave room for all possible solutions to the day's problems and catastrophes, ensuring that every possibility is explored and the best answer to our difficult problems is employed [2]. Perhaps unchecked, the free market is prone to failure and exploitation… or not. Perhaps over-zealously adopted interventionist policies can oppress or overheat a market and destroy an economy… or not. Perhaps central planning is overly complex when adopted with hopes of controlling every aspect of every life, family, and corporation… or not. *Perhaps every policy should be considered before it is totally ignored on ideological grounds…* this is my premise and there is no "or not.".

Left to reasonable rules a free market has the potential to grow indefinitely. Though fiscal policy or heavy handed regulations can cause harm, interventionist and countercyclical policy can reduce the effects of the business cycle, promote improved aggregate demand, and push nations into further eras of greater economic growth. When markets have been destroyed, have naturally failed, or have failed to emerge to begin with, sometimes only central planning can correct the failures and finally push an economy to become a global participant. Given the right conditions each argument can be relevant.

Isaac Newton's famous third law of motion, *"For every action there is an equal and opposite reaction,"* is equally applicable in economic policy making. Countries are not acting alone in some closed laboratory. There are other countries and peoples to consider when policy makers write laws. Like a game of chess, when one player makes a move, the opponent will next make a move. Good players may make logical plays while less experienced or poor players may move irrationally. A nation may opt for primarily free markets without subsidies, only to find some other nation is unfairly competing in world markets. States may decide on subsidizing one industry over another, only to discover the market was not ready for such investment and would not support the infant industry. Governments may adopt ownership over the means of production, hold on to power over production for far too long, and find their command and control system was only a temporary means to an ultimately free market end.

When considering a nation's policies, other nations' reactions cannot be ignored. Unilaterally deciding to adopt complete deregulation or absconding from world politics could be deleterious to any country's interests, economic or otherwise. Harry S. Truman once stated, *"Give me a one handed economist. All my economists say on the one hand... on the other."* His economists were probably offering him the benefits and consequences of every policy he was considering, most likely whittling his options down to two policies for consideration and no real direction. Truman may have desired a more direct answer to the problems he faced, one with fewer caveats and complications from the levers he was pulling, but his wish was even less desirable than the alternative. With a rich philosophical, economical, and geopolitical landscape, the world is an interconnected and complicated place that cannot be reduced to simple answers. Harry Truman needed a *Three-Handed Economist*.

In this book we will journey through time, trekking from Mercantilism, gold-backed currencies, laissez-faire governments and broken markets, into fiat currencies, capitalist and Marxist experimentation, and finally mixed economies and the development of impoverished nations. I will discuss how the future requires a balanced approach between freedom and regulation, free markets and socialism, and the proper mix of capitalism and government regulation within such topics as monetary policy and healthcare. Finally, I will offer a novel idea on development economics – a view on how broken markets can be repaired through the adoption of geopolitically unpopular economic policy. I will explain how we can see the logical way into the future and prosperity, if we simply remember our recent past. Sometimes the way forward is by first taking a look back.

Distant History

The Carthaginian military prepared their forces, and more than 25,000 soldiers marched into Oroscopa. They successfully repelled the Numidian invading armies and captured two of the Numidian commanders, both of whom were princes. After repeated challenges to Carthage's power from smaller, lesser-equipped, and less-powerful neighbors, Rome saw weakness in the Carthaginian Empire. Rome had been long seeking an excuse to invade, and the war between Carthage and Numidia, a Roman ally, was just what they had been searching for; they invaded shortly after.

The third Punic War began in 149 BC, two years after the attack at Oroscopa, when Carthage failed to agree to incredibly oppressive and unreasonable Roman demands. The already overbearing treaty that ended the second Punic War, forcibly mandated by the Roman Republic, had inspired zealous neighboring city-states to take advantage of the Carthaginian weakness, whittling away at Carthaginian interests, and further tempting the Roman desire for conquest, empire, and glory. Claiming lands and trade otherwise controlled by the powerful Carthage, which needed Roman permission to fight back, Roman allies were acquiring new power at a staggering rate, and Rome herself was ascending to even greater heights of power and prestige. The Carthaginian Empire, unable to fully recover from the first and second Punic Wars grasped to retain power, but soon lost its sandy economic footing. Lacking a proper military to defend its outlying settlements, a proper navy to defend its capital city (or for proper trade), and impoverished from Roman sanctions and trade restrictions, Carthage was soon placed under siege by Roman forces after submitting to Roman demands to give up what was left of their defensive weapons and fleet.

Numidian and Greek trade interests had been creeping in on Carthage for more than 100 years, and after two major wars with the Roman Republic, Carthage was in no position to continue its expansion, protect its ever-shrinking empire, or maintain its existing trade routes. The greatness of Carthage had waned, and the newfound, unchallenged power of the Roman Republic, with its powerful armies, strong navies, and reigning economic supremacy, were encroaching on all who challenged – and subsequently fell to – her legions. Rome would eventually destroy Carthage, and fearing another Carthaginian reprisal, they burned the city and its arable fields, massacred more than 450,000 Carthaginian people, and enslaved the remaining 50,000 citizens who survived. It was even rumored, though it most likely never truly occurred, that the Roman legions sowed the farmlands of Carthage with salt, thus ensuring it never reemerged as a world economic power.

From ancient civilizations to advanced economic powers such as Rome and Carthage, as nations developed and economies grew, trade routes emerged. Trade ensured more power for the elite and better standards of living for the lower classes; everyone benefitted from trade, just as they do today. Dismally, trade also ensured war would wreak havoc on the weak, since the strong would always seek more power, wealth, and prestige through conquest and acquisition.

For millennia the act of international trade, in fact all economic policy, has been subject to governmental whims, political change, and uncertainty. Though it may seem like a 20th century invention, international trade has existed almost from the beginning of humankind. Its nature has not changed greatly over the span of time, but the fast pace of today's world has certainly changed its appearance. As new methods of trade have emerged, government intervention has become more common and protectionist protocols have influenced every nation's fiscal, monetary, and trade decisions. In today's economy, exchange rates and fiat currencies rule the economic landscape, as foreign policy and treaties act to influence trade decisions and every nation reacts to every other nation's policy accords.

The history of economics is rich, interesting, intense, and diverse. For millennia nations have traded with one another, people have been subject to supply and demand forces, and corporations have tried every profit-maximizing technique they can learn. Countries jockey for economic power, claiming lands, growing into great empires and seemingly inevitably collapsing into ruin. The business cycle pushes forth, ebbing and flowing; whole societies respond with reform or revolt, and as the centuries unapologetically creep by, new nations emerge as old ones fade into history. Like nations, while under the pressure of political or ideological discord, economic policy ideas come and go as well.

Mercantilism

Mercantilism was the most accepted economic system before Adam Smith wrote his magnum opus, *An Inquiry into the Nature and Causes of the Wealth of Nations* (*Wealth of Nations*). Wishing to acquire wealth through an export-driven economic model, nations hoped to avoid the importation of foreign goods if imports outweighed the exportation of domestic goods. Through a positive balance of trade, governments believed they could acquire wealth, power, and prestige. The goal of mercantilism was to acquire as much wealth as a nation could through maximizing exports, minimizing imports, and ultimately acquiring power through riches. If a nation's government could control global trade, in turn controlling global economics, then it could shore up national security and expand its empire unchallenged. It was generally accepted that imports weakened a nation's economic status by depleting the national treasury; conversely, strength could be acquired as exports filled the treasury and enriched the nation.

Mercantilism was popular during the period ranging between the 16th and 19th centuries. Policies which highlighted mercantilism included high tariffs, trade partner restrictions, banning the export of precious metals, shipping restrictions, import quotas, and export subsidies. Almost every protectionist policy argument – infant industry, national security, trade deficits, anti-dumping – was employed during the height of mercantilism.

Nations which adopted protectionist policies, with the hope of encouraging exports and discouraging imports, unwittingly created an incentive for war. The 17th, 18th, and 19th centuries were speckled with trade-related warfare, mostly due to mercantilism. Whoever controlled key ports or key trade routes controlled the majority of trade, exports, and trade related regulation. The Anglo-Dutch Wars were fought over trade routes on at least three separate occasions. Each war lasted between two and four years, and wreaked havoc on the global economy of the era.

The first of the wars began when Great Britain mandated that all imports into England be delivered only on British ships, a protectionist policy to assist British shipping. This dictum most directly affected the Dutch, who were then targeted by pirates who used the new policy as an excuse to attack Dutch trade ships. Further exacerbating the problem, the British insisted other nation's ships "strike their flags" in salute to their fleets, even when they were in a foreign nation's port. A skirmish broke out, and the first war began a few months later when in 1652, a Dutch ship failed to strike its flag quickly enough. Eventually the British won the war – apparently they were right that the Dutch should strike their flags and their protectionist policy was justified – and a treaty heavily tilted in favor of Great Britain was signed.

The second Anglo-Dutch war was fought after King Charles of England adopted anti-Dutch mercantilist policies – under the assumption that they would increase British trade, assist shipping, heighten Britain's power in geo-politics, and increase British finances. This war instead proved harmful to the British Economy, finally forcing Britain to sign a less than desirable treaty with the Dutch. Similar protectionist policies lead to the third Anglo-Dutch war and to a similar outcome. Future wars, like The Opium Wars, were also a direct result of trade-related national policies. The British wished to export opium to China, but China, facing increasing opium addiction and the increasing drain of silver, finally issued and eventually enforced an anti-opium edict. Great Britain sent military forces to China and the Opium Wars began.

Even today, nations such as South Korea, Taiwan, Singapore, Hong Kong, and particularly China, have adopted the export-driven model. The so-called, "Asian Tigers," grew tremendously in the late 20th century and continue to do so. There is not anything inherently wrong with export-driven economies except that they are unsustainable in the long term. If every nation on earth is exporting, and none is importing, then who is buying? Furthermore, at some point a nation's people may decide to become consumers themselves, searching for decreased prices, seeking better lives, and hoping for an improved standard of living. Adopting more trade-friendly policies or free-trade agreements and focusing on a nation's comparative advantage would be better for growth in the long term. In light of the success of the Asian Tigers, new developing nations are now adopting similar export-driven, protectionist policies. Indonesia, Malaysia, the Philippines, and Thailand, are quickly becoming known as the Tiger Cub Economies as their economies pick up steam and they move headstrong into the 21st century global economy.

Free Markets – Laissez-faire Economics

Though many nations still operated under mercantilist policies throughout the 19th century, the free market and free trade ideals began to take hold. Free market policies and preferences gained much acceptance following Adam Smith's revolutionary *Wealth of Nations* and leading nations of the period began to grow more quickly than before. Regulation of local markets was relatively rare in democratic societies and following the American and French Revolutions, new, more laissez-faire approaches to government policies – such as "Mind Your Business" minted on the first American coin – were being adopted.

With their hands off the reigns of society, nations were able to make decisions about their own well-being and they had the incentive to invent and innovate. Adam Smith's "invisible hand" (described below) was working to the betterment of society, jobs were materializing as entrepreneurs were emerging, and economies began to grow. As each individual acted on their own behalf, the whole of society would reap the rewards of those actions to the betterment of entire civilizations. Since poor personal decisions, poor corporate decisions, and unethical actions would discourage members of society from doing business with other members in the society, economically active members of society were thus incentivized to undertake ethical business operations and make better personal and corporate decisions. The general wisdom that the economy would self-regulate without the need of government intervention dawned; the so-called "invisible hand" would automatically organize, coordinate, and regulate the markets without government intervention.

As time progressed free market economists realized that the government should never need to regulate the quality of goods and services, since the market would coordinate such a regulative action automatically. As the quality of a product erodes, customers will learn about the degradation of their favorite goods and simply choose not to purchase them. Without customers to purchase their goods and services, firms face an incentive to produce better products, or, facing bankruptcy, leave the market.

One may argue that customers cannot choose whether to purchase certain goods or not since goods like food and clothing are necessary for survival; thus, firms have no incentive to improve the quality of those goods. At this point a free market economist would argue that a competitive market always promotes the well-being of market participants. Seeking an economic profit, new entrepreneurs will enter the market and offer higher quality products with the hope of increasing their own market share. As their market share increases and bad firms' market shares decrease, the original firms face the incentive to either supply more preferable/better quality goods or go bankrupt when they are unable to sell their existing substandard products. Furthermore, as more firms enter the market and compete against existing firms, prices will begin to fall, making goods more affordable for everyone. Prices decline, quality rises, and consumers benefit.

It is also unnecessary for governments to control the production plans of a nation's industries. Market forces are more effective and efficient than any central planner could ever be. The supply and demand forces within the economy itself will do the regulation automatically, as existing goods are sold in the market and new goods are manufactured to take their place. When supplies are low, suppliers have a profit incentive to supply more of that good. Therefore, when shelves run low, the entrepreneur becomes aware that more product is needed and orders replacement goods. Producers then manufacture and ship replacement goods and refill the shelves with the needed items. If supplies are too high suppliers will have clearance sales to reduce their stocks, reduce future orders for goods, and mitigate or eliminate future surpluses. The government does not need to intervene since the markets automatically coordinate this activity.

Finally, the government does not need to regulate prices, and even price gouging is a logical fallacy. An equilibrium state, where supply is equal to demand, will always self-emerge within any market economy. The laws of supply and demand will always regulate the economy, without intervention from any central planner; this is an axiom. When the price of a good is high, the quantity demanded will be low; when the price of a good is low, the quantity demanded will be high. Alternatively, when the price of a good is high, the quantity of the good supplied will be high; when the price of a good is low, the quantity of the good supplied will be low. If the price is too high, more will be supplied than is demanded and a surplus will occur, thus pressuring the price downward and back toward equilibrium – this we regularly witness through clearance sales, blue light specials, seasonal discounts, etc. If the price of a good is too low, demand will outweigh supply, a shortage will occur, thus pressuring the price upward and back toward equilibrium – this we regularly witness through the price of gasoline every time there is a war in the Middle East, a hurricane in the Gulf of Mexico, or any other of a myriad of supply side shocks. No government intervention is needed; markets will self-calibrate.

There are always those who claim that various events, like natural disasters, require government intervention in the markets. They claim that unethical shysters will gouge customers on prices and take advantage of a horrible situation. A free market economist, however, would see this gouging (from a purely economic standpoint) as a natural state of affairs, and an opportunity for the market to help those in need by coordinating economic activity to the benefit of those in need. A market void has appeared, and market forces would have a chance to fill the gap.

Assume for a moment that a hurricane destroys much of your town, and that government help will not fill the need for water for several days, perhaps a week. (In fact, under an entirely free market regime the government would not provide any aid, not even supplies of desperately needed water.) Seven days without a proper supply for water means the death toll would be enormous. However, with a profit incentive, various entrepreneurs may fill box trucks and deliver the water to those in need – for the right price. Perhaps they sell the water for $10 per bottle, a ridiculous price to be certain, but no water means certain death so $10 becomes acceptable. Other entrepreneurs learn of the profit to be earned and, motivated by the dream for riches, they fill their own trucks and deliver even more water to the affected area. Supplies begin to rise, prices begin to fall, and before too long the price of water is back to normal and the potentially enormous death toll is averted. Price-gouging entrepreneurs leave the affected areas, and normal supply levels and access to supply chains once again take hold.

Alternatively, and under current laws, the government declares your town or state as a disaster area, and fearing government reprisal and possible jail time, nobody brings water; no heroes appear over the horizon. A shortage occurs, and many go without or resort to drinking contaminated water. The contaminated water makes people sick from water-borne pathogens, and without proper medical care, those affected may even die. Those that go without have about three days, perhaps four, before they too must face the possibility of death. I will leave it to you to decide which scenario is better, to have water for $10 per bottle or not to have water at all.

The above story occurred in 1992, when Hurricane Andrew devastated Florida and many other parts of the United States. It happened again in 2005 when Hurricane Katrina destroyed much of the gulf coast. Many suffered the consequences of the government not reacting fast enough to help. Many also suffered the consequences of an overly reactive police force, when the government unfortunately did react fast enough to stop profiteers from filling the dire need.

For fairness I should mention it is possible the free market would not react quickly enough either. It could take several days for profiteers or volunteer organizations to collect supplies, get time off work, and drive to the affected areas. Today, however, it is not profiteers who flow into areas of need; it is aid agencies, and they move fast. I was chasing the tornado that ravaged Joplin, MO in 2011, and I drove into the devastated city only moments after the storm passed. There was nothing left except piles of rubble and people who were buried alive. Like ants from a hill, people quickly surfaced to assist in search and rescue, and hundreds of lives were saved as a result.

The government-led response was also swift and rescuers were able to limit the death toll to 161 lost lives – making it the third most deadly tornado in U.S. history, but it could easily have been the first. Nearby cities and neighboring communities heroically came to Joplin's assistance within hours, Aid agencies were there within two days, and the need for manpower and supplies was met with excess. This is precisely the argument, however. Even if the government workers had not been there, the aid agencies, local citizens, and neighboring communities would have been. There was no need to regulate prices on supplies because the market was met with an abundance of free items. Even if profiteers had arrived on the scene, price gouging would have been impossible since would-be gougers would have had to compete with free aid.[3]

---

[3] As I wrote the above paragraph my thoughts were with Moore, OK. Growing up in the Midwest everyone knows during tornado season it is possible one's home or town could be hit. Yet it is still a surprise when one's home town is ravaged by Mother Nature. I wish all those affected by natural disasters peace of mind and a quick return to abundance.

Gilded Age and Industrialists – the Robber Barons

Filling a dire need in the short term, when there is an expectation for normal pricing and supply chains to return within a few weeks or months is arguably acceptable. However, taking advantage of an open and free market where no such expectation exists is what we have termed the Gilded Age of Industrialism and is arguably unethical and possibly immoral. The Gilded Age is a time in American and European history when many entrepreneurs emerged, created millions of jobs, and accelerated many nations down the road to greatness, including the United States – but that growth came with costs.

Macroeconomic theory and most textbooks on the subject, postulate that incentives are incredibly important and conclude that ambition and creativity can be stifled when incentive for innovation or invention is in some way inhibited. Without the industrialists, investment into highly productive manufacturing may never have materialized, and nations may have suffered from fewer jobs for their citizens. Economies may have grown much slower, standards of living may not have risen as far as they have, and the industrial revolution may never have begun. Without a profit motive, James Watt may never have had a reason to invent the steam engine. When no motivation exists, entire societies suffer, and, without profit, entire societies stagnate. Free from overbearing regulation, however, the industrial revolution did occur. Though the growing pangs were long and robust, our nation emerged far stronger. Unfortunately, though, many endured much hardship from industrialist greed along the way. Profit is the catalyst to greatness but also the impetus to ruin.

The industrialists, known by the derogatory term of "Robber Barons,", grew immensely wealthy as they exploited labor for cash, grew their empires, and were themselves an unstoppable economic force. The Robber Barons' goals rarely included the betterment of society, although it was often a side effect; they were mostly motivated by selfish gain, pride, and profit [3]. Furthermore, they often operated outside or above the law of the land.

During the Gilded Age the standard of living for many did not improve; in fact it eroded. Various Robber Barons took advantage of the virtually indentured American worker, employing harsh working conditions and lax safety standards. Work-related injuries and death were common, and men found themselves indebted to company stores in company towns, paid with company money called scrip (wages redeemable only at company stores owned by the corporation employing the workers) instead of American cash, and their debt to the company often grew beyond their wages. Unable to escape the reality of debt to the company and with little to no government issued cash to begin life anew, workers were often enslaved within an inescapable cycle of poverty and ruin.

It was common for workers to work six and sometimes seven days in a week, often 12-hour shifts, and rarely, if ever, receiving breaks. Overtime pay was not required by law, so corporations simply had no incentive to pay it. Corporate owners understood that if workers quit their jobs, there were many other unemployed workers eager to fill those positions. Furthermore, mistreated workers knew that quitting work could possibly mean starvation for their family and eviction from their home when they were unable to gain new employment. Facing the real possibility of homelessness, and the reality that the vast majority of production work existed under terrible conditions, workers encountered an impossible decision. Quitting one job because of bad working conditions often meant accepting another with similar or worse dangers and environments. Facing the prospect of ruin, in a time when finding a new job was not as simple as turning on a computer, workers inevitably chose to endure the harsh working conditions.

It is often forgotten that unions emerged to fulfill a great need that the free, unregulated market had ignored. Free market economists almost always ignore that unions were a free market creation in which where a single worker did not have market power – but a union did. Various worker uprisings occurred, and many workers eventually organized and finally began to unionize. As unions organized and gained market power, men such as Henry Clay Frick, responded to their demands for shorter workdays, safer working conditions, and better pay, by breaking up unions instead of negotiating with them. Change rarely comes easy, however; and, in time, the unions would fulfill their purpose.

Frick, who was chairman of the Carnegie Steel Company in 1892, became famous for provoking his workers into a strike and subsequently declaring war on them. Worker strikes were occurring all over the country, and Frick wagered it was only a matter of time before it happened at his plants. The Homestead Strike, as it was later known, occurred after Frick had correctly anticipated worker complaints and then proceeded to provoke them into a strike by working them longer and harder than before. He was successful when workers finally organized a strike, refused to work, and barricaded themselves in front of the factory, blocking any entry into the facility, completely halting factory production. Frick responded by building a wooden wall around the striking workers – who affectionately dubbed the fortified mill "Fort Frick" – and calling in the Pinkerton detectives. The Pinkertons were given Winchester rifles and placed on two nearby barges so they could attack the trapped workers from the water. Nine workers were killed during the skirmish before the state militia intervened and stopped the violence. A later attempt on Frick's life would prove unsuccessful, and following the murderous event, neither he nor the Pinkerton detectives were ever charged with a crime.

Although great leaps in manufacturing and production were realized, and our infrastructure and transportation systems were revolutionized as a result of the Robber Barrons' intervention, many misfortunes occurred because of their existence. We remember names such as Cornelius Vanderbilt and John D. Rockefeller and their large empires. We admire men such as Henry Ford and Andrew Carnegie for their creative innovations and philanthropy. There is no doubt that many people played great roles in creating and improving the American economy through the industrial revolution. However, the Gilded Age was tarnished by forgotten iniquities which stemmed from a lack of regulation. The free unregulated market's amoral side was crowned by the Robber Barons' debauchery. We often forget the deep depravity of the men or their associates whom we admire, but our history proves that some regulation is certainly a necessity.

Free Market and Labor Regulation

The Gilded Age lasted from 1865 to roughly 1900, and though the nation grew faster than it had ever grown before, many evils occurred – all of which could have been avoided by simple government intervention. An exploited populous sometimes has little choice but to accept terrible working conditions, little pay, or a dangerous working environment. The labor force and the demand for employment of that age were both relatively inelastic; thus, the labor force was easily exploitable. It can take decades for an over-exploited workforce to organize and prevent further abuse, but it only takes a few months to write a bill and have it signed into law. The unregulated free market is ripe for exploitation and it is the responsibility of the government to act once free market weaknesses are made evident.

The labor force included men, women, and children in 1890. The claim of free market economists is that innovation emerges to fill needs as they become evident, and child labor was a free market solution in the absence of government intervention. By the year 1900, children accounted for approximately 18% of the entire labor supply in a wide array of dirty and dangerous jobs; in fact, over 1.7 million children even worked in coal mines! The problem only grew with the invention of the sewing machine, since many children were then employed as weavers or lace makers. When productivity slowed, the children, after hours of being bent over a table and tired from working, were often beaten as punishment or to improve productivity. Worse conditions existed in factories, where children were precariously exposing themselves to constant danger and injury while employed to sweep floors or keep factories clean. Children were also utilized to work in match factories where they were highly likely to see their teeth rot out, and possibly succumb to disease, permanent disability from chemical exposure, or death. Many were hired for more physical industrial work where they were often trapped, maimed, or crushed to death as they crawled under machines to clean gears and do simple repairs, or were expected to squeeze into small spaces to retrieve lost tools or materials. Rather than the free market solving this problem with more accessible machines, non-abuse policies, or safer working conditions, industrialists simply neglected the issue entirely, exposing children and workers to horribly dangerous conditions.

The free, unregulated market allowed many to gain employment and a wealthier lot in life – actually, real wages (pay in terms of buying power) increased by more than 50% from 1860 to 1890 [4] – but conditions endangered many workers. Lack of regulation allowed logical safety and sanitation measures to be ignored in the interest of decreased costs and increased profit. Workers suffered the consequences of cost-saving actions adopted by greedy leadership. As the Gilded Age progressed, various states passed laws enforcing factory inspection and safety standards or guidelines, but states lacked proper funding for regulators so the laws were rarely enforced and largely ignored.

From 1880 to 1900, an average of about 35,000 workers died in industrial accidents every year, and another 500,000 were injured [5]. When unions finally emerged to demand better working conditions and shorter workdays, the government often intervened – on behalf of the *corporations*. Presidents sometimes even utilized federal troops to stop union organization – like during the Great Railroad Strike of the 1870's. Courts ordered the breakup of unions which had justified complaints – like during the Pullman Strike of 1894. Factory leadership, like in the Anthracite Coal Strike, often ignored demands for negotiated settlement, and unions were powerless to stop the many abuses propagated by corporations who were, far too often, protected by the government. Similar government intervention against unions is occurring today, leading some economists like Robert Reich to claim we are entering, or are already in, a modern gilded age.

Eventually, while court action and presidential authority mitigated unions' real coercive power and demand for change, state leadership and congress finally began acting to protect the American worker. The Bureau of Labor was established under the department of the Interior in 1888, and though it did not accomplish much, it was a very important step in the right direction. Government regulations that could have saved lives, prevented strikes, and promoted more effective growth were finally being adopted after decades of obvious need. In 1903, under President Theodore Roosevelt, the Department of Commerce and Labor was established, illuminating change just over the horizon.

In 1916 the government finally mandated an eight-hour workday with the passing of the Adamson Act. The act only addressed specific industries, but it was another step down the road toward employee protections. Industrialists were outraged and sued for the law to be overturned. The case, Wilson v. New, eventually made it to the U.S. Supreme Court where it was found to be constitutional. A few years later a 40-hour workweek was established in the Fair Labor Standards Act of 1938, and OSHA was eventually created to address worker safety in 1970. It took over 100 years for the government to legislate what the free market never solved – in fact refused to solve – on its own.

Other Necessary Regulations

One may still argue that the free market, though slow, is effective at self-regulating. The questions remain: At what cost is the slow reaction of the free market too high? When is the free market, though effective, simply too slow? I often consider statistics such as a 1:1,000,000 chance and how certain events are very unlikely to occur. When I experienced the F-5 tornado that ravaged Joplin, MO in 2011, I later considered the odds of its occurrence in any specific location – namely Joplin, MO. I have lived through several tornadoes in my life, but the statistics state – unless I am chasing tornadoes – that being in more than one tornado is an almost impossibility. Mathematically, the probability can justifiably be rounded to zero!

It does not matter what the statistics are if you are the one that is affected, especially if the negative effects could have been avoided by your proactive action, or in the case of our economy, proactive government action. Should the free market be allowed to experiment for 10 years, or 20 years, or 50 years before market forces finally remove threats or improve conditions for the masses? No. When it is entirely possible the free market will refuse to address the issue at hand, the government can quickly observe the threat and react far more effectively. More importantly, the government can react far more quickly and mitigate the negative effects for market participants before they are harmed through the slow-moving, self-regulation of markets.

It is often stated that government intervention in favor of the environment is a waste of taxpayer money, that the Food and Drug Administration (FDA) is unnecessary, and that many other executive branch agencies and legislative interventions are extraneous in the presence of a free market. These arguments ignore certain facts about our consumer base, irrational choices, and the population's knowledge. The consumer base is large and consumers are largely uninformed about the operation of markets or the goods they consume. Even with the advent of the internet, and the availability of information at our fingertips, our population remains, sadly, largely oblivious to information it needs to make "rational" choices. Perhaps because of the availability of information, everyone simply assumes they will know when firms discount sustainable activities, adopt destructive habits, or ignore public health hazards; unfortunately, these assumptions are usually incorrect in the presence of profit-maximizing corporations. Additionally, consumers are often not wealthy enough to purchase alternatives even when they are aware of heinous corporate activity.

Whether one believes in human caused or natural climate change, everyone can agree they like clean air and clean water; so if addressing climate change makes our environment cleaner, then let's get to it already. The Environmental Protection Agency (EPA) was created in 1970, more than 100 years after the start of the Gilded Age. It was created in response to the ever increasing need to ensure the environment was clean and habitable, since corporations were ignoring their own negative impacts on the environment. In that era it was not uncommon for corporations to dump waste into waterways or toxic gases into our atmosphere and air – in fact corporations still ignore the consequences of those activities in developing nations such as China where they can produce more competitively and at lower monetary costs by ignoring environmental consequences. The EPA is actively engaged in the protection of our environment, and has repeatedly enacted continually steeper rules for clean air and water since its inception. In 1971 the EPA enacted a restriction on lead-based paint, something the free market had ignored, and facing few other options the population continued to purchase these products even though the toxic effects on children were well known [6]. In 1972 the EPA banned the use of DDT, a common pesticide known to contribute to the growth of cancers but still used in both public and private spaces; in fact, it is still utilized as pesticide in many developing nations since it is less expensive than safer options. In the same year the EPA further addressed problems the free market had ignored and mandated the nationwide creation of a far more efficient and cleaner sewage treatment system. This system was finally completed in 1988, and ultimately stopped the disposal of sewage into public waterways that were often utilized for public drinking water. The developing nations of the world still suffer from the lack of a proper sanitation and waste disposal system. Their markets are not addressing the problem, and their governments do not have the funds.

The list continues in 1973 when the EPA limited factory disposal of pollutants into waterways, and began a systematic phase out of lead in gasoline, two more protections the free market had previously ignored. Later, after discovering sulfur was causing acid rain in Europe, diesel-producing companies were mandated to remove sulfur from their fuels. Further actions ranging from clean air, clean water, hazardous waste and more have continued throughout the EPA's existence and still continue today. Would the free market have eventually addressed these public health concerns? Most likely yes, but, evident from its own history of environmental neglect, certainly not before many people were already experiencing the negative health effects caused by that neglect.

Today we can simply observe the developing world and witness the health effects of such environmental neglect – particularly China. Many Chinese waterways are now so contaminated that the water is undrinkable and barely able to be purified, and the air in some major cities is so polluted that healthy people begin to cough within minutes of disembarking at the airports. When the weather turns cold, China is known to suffer from smog so thick that work is sometimes cancelled and visibility can decline to as low as 10 meters. I have spoken with Chinese exchange students who report a yellow sky in Beijing, instead of blue as one might expect. Before the year 2000 it was very rare for Chinese citizens to be diagnosed with cancer; today, due to a lack of enforced environmental regulations, the Chinese government has even admitted to the existence of entire "cancer villages" in their large nation [7] .

The Food and Drug Administration (FDA) was officially created in 1930, but can trace its origins back to 1906 with the passing of the Pure Food and Drugs Act, also known as the Wiley Act. The Wiley Act prohibited interstate commerce in adulterated and misbranded food and drugs. No law protecting consumers had been passed before the passing of the Wiley Act, and since its passing the FDA has continued its role in consumer protection. The FDA has come a long way since its inception and now ensures various drugs are the doses they say and foods are what they claim. In fact, had the FDA existed when the X-Ray was created and utilized for activities ranging from checking the correct fit of shoes, to the removal of unwanted hair, many cancers and deaths may well have been avoided.

In 2008 the FDA became involved with stopping the Chinese Baby Milk Scandal from charging our shores. Chinese manufactures had been manufacturing baby formula and mixing it with a substance called melamine. Melamine, essentially a plastic that is very difficult to detect without specifically searching for it, was causing kidney stones in Chinese babies. The tainted baby food was traced to over 54,000 infants in China being hospitalized with severe kidney stones and 13 deaths due to malnutrition [8]. Luckily, the FDA halted the imports of Chinese-made baby formula and protected the American public from the present danger. Less than a month later, the FDA stopped further shipments of different baby foods from China that were found to contain carcinogens. While the Chinese officials wrestle with criminalizing such horrible market activities, the FDA has helped protect the American public at large from imported baby food to pet food. Other nations, such as Australia, were not as lucky.

Certain substances (often addictive) are also regulated by the Food and Drug Administration. Ephedrine is no longer available over-the-counter in the United States, for example. Ephedrine is a substance with side effects that are known to be dangerous, and the previous lack of regulation lead to inconsistent doses in over-the-counter ephedrine pills. Some doses were very high, leading to heart attacks, strokes, and even death, while other doses were relatively safe for consumption or so low as to be ineffective. Anyone wishing to stay awake and alert would certainly consider the use of these previously unregulated drugs.

However, consumers rarely do their due diligence or investigation and simply accept the signals markets provide. Perhaps peer pressure, perhaps pretty packaging, perhaps price point, but consumers often choose poorly and sometimes pay with their health, or worse. Unfortunately, many products have a constantly changing consumer base, which leads to their perpetual existence even when they obtain a poor reputation. If a company's reputation suffers enough, it is not difficult for them to re-label or reincorporate under a different name and continue their market activities as if no issues had ever occurred. The free market has no recourse for such behavior if corporations are left unregulated. Next time you are in the store and considering the purchase of a drug or supplement that says it has not been evaluated by the FDA, think twice before you make the purchase.

Other governmental organizations exist to regulate various other activities. A clear example that is closer to home is that of drunk driving. We all know it is a bad decision to drink and then to drive. Yet every year drunk drivers kill thousands of people. Left unregulated, the number of deaths related to inebriation would almost certainly be far greater. How many of us have known people that visited a bar and then drove home three sheets to the wind? It is possible they made it home safely, but how many of us have known someone who was killed by a drunk driver? Should our roads be deregulated and traffic laws be eliminated? Of those whom we have known to drive drunk, I think we can safely assume they were not concerned about dying, nor that they will kill someone else; they were concerned about the size of the ticket, or possibly the jail time they might receive if they were caught.

The penalties for drunk driving, and the risk of getting caught, are often high enough to discourage or stop someone from making such a poor decision. Drunk drivers rarely considers the possible death sentence they might receive, not from the law but from the accident they might encounter. Left to an unregulated market, and the misleading thoughts that it "won't happen to me," the roadways would almost certainly be far more dangerous. The free market solution is a bit ridiculous; if one is afraid or believes the risk from drunk drivers is too high, then just do not drive anywhere. The free market solution to many economic questions is sometimes impossible, often implausible, and frequently impractical.

The FDA also regulates much of our food quality, although the USDA regulates the quality of meat. A few years ago Taco Bell was accused of selling beef that did not even qualify as meat according to USDA standards [9]. After issuing statements defending its products, arguing against the evidence, and claiming its food was a proprietary blend, it became clear that Taco Bell would have continued its misleading practice in the absence of outside intervention and regulation. However, when the USDA learned of the transgression, the fast food chain quickly corrected the problem. A failure of market forces became evident when demand for the food did not decline, and following the correction the company's sales quickly returned to normal and its consumer base continued to grow. Most recently the same company has recalled products found to contain horse meat, and in Iceland, officials have found beef products with no meat at all! Would the free market have provided a solution to this sort of activity? For this one, I must conclude it would not.

Many companies claim they can cure cancer, many doctors make the same claim, and many get wealthy from the false hope they offer. Some companies know of failures and argue over who is responsible, like during the Firestone-Ford tire recall in the year 2000. Ultimately, even amongst all the negative press, Firestone and Ford both emerged more profitable and more popular after the recall efforts. In fact, I worked at Firestone just after the recall and most of the managers claimed sales had actually increased. Tires had become a short term loss-leader for vehicle inspections which lead to other, sometimes more expensive, repairs! The free market certainly works, but without government oversight it is prone to temptation and exploitation.

I must state, when consumers make bad decisions based on laziness or apathy, I share no sympathy for their pain. However, I also believe it is the responsibility of the government to protect its citizens. It is the job of the firm to sell, the job of the citizen to produce, and whether it be from outside threat of harm or terror, internal threat from profiteering and false signals, inexperience, or apathy, it is the job of the government to protect. While the unbridled free market may eventually act on our behalf, it may take too long, if it reacts at all, and the price we will pay for the delay will always be too high. While the government may utilize an overly active (or even proactive) and ultra-conservative bureau like the FDA, it is better to be too safe than be harmed by the inaction of a benevolent government and an amoral free market.

Government Failures and Commanding Heights

The term "Commanding Heights" originated in a speech by Vladimir Lenin. He was referring to specific sectors of the economy that he believed the government should control. Industries related to energy, transportation, banking, and mining are included in Lenin's idea of the Commanding Heights. For example, Lenin believed it was important for the government to control the steel industry for national security and modernization. He ignored innovations the private markets would make and the advancements the profit incentive could foster. Too much government command and control leads to inefficiencies, and ultimately failure of the economy at large.

Central planning of major industries is very difficult to accomplish effectively, and control over minor markets and entrepreneurs further complicates the central command and control system. The United States does not have a "Commanding Heights" economy, but the mixed economy we do have teeters on the edge of command and control as bureaus continually grow larger and sometimes adopt oppressive regulations. As these bureaus constantly lobby for more funding and more manpower they often grow beyond what is necessary. Exacerbating the problem, once bureaus receive initial funding they are often difficult or politically impossible to eliminate. After all, though it is the job of a bureau to regulate its respective field, it must ensure its continued existence through constant growth and increased funding or it risks outliving its usefulness. By promoting the perception of need, bureaus perpetually justify their existence and continued expansion. As a result of our mixed system led by bureaucracies, our government continues to grow ever larger.

When governments fail, they fail spectacularly. When the free market fails, it usually fails with a whimper. Therefore, state intervention is not always the answer either. There are plenty of examples of government failures in the world economy. Poor central planning can lead to over corrections and unmitigated disasters. It may take the free market decades to self-correct (or to fail), but it takes only a few years for a government failure to become evident, and only a few strokes of a pen for a government to adopt disastrous policy with almost immediate negative effects. It is important to note, however, that when a government fails through incorrectly anticipating the state of the economy it is often able to make adjustments and corrections far more reactively than the slow, even if adaptive, free market. Alternatively, though, when a government fails through incorrectly anticipating the state of the economy it often pays for the mistake with people's well-being, and sometimes their lives.

After the Chinese Revolution, Mao Zedong believed he could modernize his nation through state ownership over steel. By doubling steel production, Mao wished to push China into a new era of world supremacy and prosperity. The over-zealous plan, the "Great Leap Forward," shifted workers from agricultural products and into steel production, which resulted in a two year famine that scholars estimate killed between 15 and 43 million people, making it the largest famine in world history [10]. Such actions by the free market, namely that of inefficient allocation of labor, would have led either to greater efficiency in production through innovation, firms migrating into different markets or simply into bankruptcy, but probably not human tragedy. (A counter-example to this would be the Dust Bowl during the Great Depression. Left unhindered, the free market allowed farmers to over-till the land and create an agricultural catastrophe that was only fixed after government intervention. The cost to public health, lives, and the economy before the government intervened, however, was high).

Government intervention proved disastrous to the people of China at the time. It is important to note that today, however, China is the world's leading steel producing nation, so Mao's forward thinking did pay off in the long term, even though it cost far too many Chinese lives. As far as efficiency, though, China utilizes 24-36% more energy than the United States to produce comparable quantities of steel, and it utilizes far more manpower [11]. China is currently undergoing a privatization of the steel industry and cuts to some factories are estimated to reduce the work force by five out of every six workers, while maintaining current levels of production. If government operation over the steel industry was efficient, then a cut of that magnitude would never be needed when it finally does privatize. Such overkill on labor does imply our work weeks could possibly be shorter to accomplish the production levels necessary for our existing standard of living.

Necessity

Some aspects of any nation should be controlled by the government but certainly not all. In the past, many nations have struggled to claim what they believe to be the property of government over market participants. The free market is very efficient in the management and transport of goods and at mining ore, for example, but the government is not. The government is very good at building roads and highways, however, and the market typically is not. It also makes sense to have limited or mixed government involvement where the free market falls short of efficient self-regulation, for the benefit of society. Most aspects of an economy should be left for private enterprise, particularly because private ownership faces incentives that governments do not face, mainly that of earning a profit. By controlling costs, businesses can operate more effectively, expand more rapidly, and innovate more readily, and it can all be done without government "red tape." Greater efficiency benefits every citizen on Earth by increasing creature comforts, improving working conditions, and through an overall improvement in society's standard of living. Businesses that are in the business of being in business instead of profit maximizing – like the government – do not remain businesses for long. Yet bureaucracies within governments seem to operate with three mandates just for that purpose: exist, operate, and grow to ensure continued existence.

Milton Friedman summed up the necessity of government most effectively when he wrote, *"government is essential both as a forum for determining the 'rules of the game' and as an umpire to interpret and enforce the rules decided on. What the market does is to reduce greatly the range of issues that must be decided through political means, and thereby to minimize the extent to which government need participate directly in the game"* [12]. In other words, government involvement in the market is a necessary evil for regulating industrial activity and mitigating market abuse, but the government should not advocate the wishes of society since markets will automatically organize those wishes, thereby limiting the need for government involvement.

Conclusion

The argument, both for and against government involvement in business and an obvious two handed approach, is compelling. So, what about the third hand of economics? There are thousands of industries that should be privately held, but mixed government involvement in two industries – banking and healthcare – is necessary, and regulation over the rest is essential; so, government bureaucracy seems truly to be a necessary evil. Free market forces should be unhindered when market conditions are natural, government regulation is prudent when markets fail or become corrupt, and government ownership in particular industries can offer assurances the public sometimes needs during times of economic hardship or crisis. One can even argue that government ownership and market involvement can sometimes be necessary under the right conditions, but only if they are limited to a short period of time, an argument I will make in chapter five.

Chapter 2: The Need for Central Banking

"There is scarcely any point in the economy of national affairs of greater moment than the uniform preservation of the intrinsic value of the money unit..."

– Alexander Hamilton

Introduction

Though the Federal Reserve (FED) failed its first major test after its creation in 1913 – namely that of poor monetary policy leading up to, during, and perhaps perpetuating the Great Depression, if not also causing it – government involvement in banking finally led to an improved banking system with less systemic risk. Banking in the United States and other nations should certainly continue to be at least partially government controlled, and we would likely see great benefits in the long term with a state owned and controlled healthcare system. The mixed ownership model of the FED, discussed in this chapter, could easily be adopted by our healthcare system, discussed in chapter three. To understand why it is necessary to employ a central bank that is separate from the central government but not entirely private or publicly owned, we must first begin with a brief history of world monetary policies.

Debasing the Currency

Governments have controlled their money at almost all points in history. Although much trading early in human history was through barter, eventually peoples realized they could simplify trade through a common currency which has varied from shells, to rocks, to precious metals, to paper, and now to electronic data. As early borders emerged and tribes aligned into cities, states, and nations, currency has most frequently settled to the use of precious metals that were cast by government mints; limited by availability there was no real need for a central authority to control their quantity and inflation usually remained low. Less common metals, like gold and silver, became the most valuable traded moneys of almost all nations, although bronze, copper, and nickel have also been used [13].

As time progressed and nations' populations grew but precious metal reserves remained relatively constant, it became evident that larger quantities of money were necessary to maintain the status quo. Furthermore, rulers wished for increased wealth and prestige. Easy money in place of taxes, along with price ceilings – like in the Roman Empire [14] – provided a tool for that purpose. These reasons, among others, lead to currency debasement. Debasing a currency occurs when a nation melts less abundant precious metals and mixes them with more abundant common metals to create impure coinage. Debasement has historically occurred when the ruling class of the nation wished to spend more money than it had in its coffers; through debasement, governments could easily create more short term spending power.

Whether it is for war, social programs, or prestige, governments frequently debase their currencies. As leadership chooses to debase, nations' currencies lose value and prices eventually begin to rise. Further temptation, inspired by a desperate need after prices rise due to the easy creation of less valuable but more abundant money, leads to further debasement of currencies – and a vicious cycle ensues. We should conclude then that even precious metals are rather arbitrary when it comes to retaining value, an idea I will discuss later in this chapter.

Ancient Rome was famous for its debasement of currency, reducing silver coins from almost pure, early in the empire, to roughly 60% silver over the course of the empire. In need of a more available common currency, the Roman central government also allowed localities to mint their own coins as long as they were not minted from precious metals. This kept monetary policy in the hands of the nation's central government, though it did not keep rulers from simply commissioning the creation of more money to pay the empire's bills, which were significant.

Perhaps the ultimate debasement occurred when governments adopted fiat currency. Fiat currency has no intrinsic value, since it can only be used to increase the convenience of trade and is a poor store of value if the government adopts irresponsible monetary policy. Strangely enough, a sort of debasement can still occur today through the printing of new money by governments or central banks – a practice most commonly undertaken during times of war, recession, or upheaval. Adopting expansionary monetary policies and printing more money as it is needed is always a great temptation to those in power. Sometimes expansionary policy can be good for an economy – as it surely would have been before the stock market crash in 1929 – but at other times it can be bad, and perfect timing is absolutely essential.

Forecasting the economy to make the correct decision on expanding the money supply must be done far in advance, sometimes six months or more is needed, and it can have dire consequences if the predictions are wrong or the timing is off. Expand the money supply when economic forecasts are correct and a recession may be averted. Modify the money supply when economic forecasts are incorrect and a period of inflation or deflation is likely to occur. Changing the money supply when forecasts are correct but a natural correction has already taken root and the boom or bust of the business cycle may only be exasperated. Finally, it is possible that the forecasts are correct and the timing is perfect, but the expansion or contraction of money in the markets is too little to help, or so high that it sows the seeds for the next expansionary bubble.

Monetary policy is difficult to time, difficult to measure, and difficult to adopt effectively. Since faith in a nation's currency is absolutely integral to the power of monetary policy and national stability, central authority – outside the pressures of political whims – is necessary for its management. Though there may be times to expand or contract the monetary base within an economy, two things are always certain: it is necessary to keep strong checks and balances on a nation's monetary policy, and it is imperative to keep the nation's politicians' power over the monetary printing press at an absolute minimum, preferably zero. This is one reason I always argue in favor of the continued existence of the Federal Reserve.

Gold Backed Currency

Although gold-backed currency is a popular idea today, commodity-backed trading has not existed for several decades. Various transaction costs are high – for example the expense in transporting large quantities of heavy gold, or worse, a ship full of gold sinking – and new methods of trade have been adopted as a result (actually there are even international pressures which resulted in our leaving the gold standard [15]). The U.S. was the last nation in the world to leave the gold-standard under President Nixon, in 1971. The history of the gold standard is often ignored by proponents of a new gold-standard today, but by remembering history we can prevent repeating the dangers our nation and the world faced at the time of the gold-standard's abandonment.

Gold emerged as a standard unit of monetary exchange because of its widespread acceptance across the world. Essentially, it was a single currency with a limited supply, no central authority, and universal acceptance, which kept it regulated automatically. Prices in terms of gold could remain relatively constant across markets, so the claim is that the gold-standard virtually eliminated inflationary pressures – although inflationary pressures were still present, and markets were still volatile. In 1844 Great Britain adopted a gold-backed paper currency, allowing the creation of money that could be spent or exchanged for its equivalent in gold; paper money reduced transaction costs and improved the convenience of trade. Most other nations of the world followed this example and also adopted a gold-standard, making exchange rates simpler and international trade easier. Throughout history various nations emerged as global currency leaders, and Great Britain, the strongest nation on earth in 1844, obtained a reserve currency status. The reserve currency status allowed Great Britain to adopt a fractional reserve system, whereby it could circulate more paper money than it actually had gold reserves to pay for. In other words, it could not retire all the debt it would acquire if other nations began exchanging their sterling notes for gold.

Under the new scheme of a gold-backed currency, Great Britain was able to attain power and prestige with greater simplicity. When it, like other nations before, realized it could still devalue its currency through simply printing more paper notes, that policy too was sometimes adopted to finance wars or other expenditures. Even under the gold-standard, the government of

Great Britain could call the presses into action and gain a temporary increase in wealth through the printing of new money. It could trade the future value on currency for current consumption of goods and services. Only after a short period of expansionary monetary policy would prices finally begin to rise, but by printing new money and devaluing existing money, Great Britain was able to borrow from itself by weakening its own currency, enabling the country to pay debts and retain power with its new, less valuable money. Simply through changing the exchange rate of currency to gold, any nation could change its quantity of currency and print more; since price changes will always lag behind a change in monetary policy, nations can always attain a short term improvement of their current fiscal or monetary situation [16].

Confederate Temptation

Nations have always been tempted to inflate their debts away. If it was not Rome, it was Persia [17]. If France needed money, creation of a speculative bubble through expansionary policy could be the answer [18]. When Great Britain fell on hard times, it fired up the presses. It is far too tempting for a nation's politically powerful or elite to have power over its money. Printing money seems like a great way to increase financial capital, and politicians rarely understand the consequences of monetary policy changes. Certainly the aggregate demand of a nation can be increased through the printing of money, but this is only a temporary measure that usually has disastrous after effects that can last years or even decades, and a gold standard does little to prevent such erroneous policies when they go wrong.

During the Civil War, both the Union States of America and the Confederate States of America needed money. The problem for each was unique, but it was far worse for the Confederacy which had enacted disastrous international trade policies. The Industrial Revolution had begun, and the Confederate economy, dependent on agricultural exports, had waned in the wake of a self-imposed embargo on cotton exports [19]. The Confederacy had hoped to pressure European powers into recognizing its legitimacy as a nation and to acquire diplomatic recognition, thereby strengthening their economy for the Confederate war effort. The embargo had the opposite effect, and the original plan to finance the war through tariffs on imports and taxes on exports was no longer viable. The Confederacy was also enduring a lasting blockade from northern forces, so the South truly had very little actual ability to tax or tariff even in the absence of the embargo. Furthermore, private financing of the war had also dried up, since southern investors – whose wealth was dependent on exports – were no longer able to donate to the cause. War taxes and various other methods of finance also failed, and the South was finally forced to either suspend war operations or to finance the effort through expansionary monetary policy.

Though the North did experience some inflation due to war spending, it was not to the extent the South had experienced. The Union's economy was as strong as ever and getting stronger, though it too would have suffered greatly if the war had lasted much longer. As the war progressed, the North was able to tax exports and tariff imports just as the South had planned. Recognized as a legitimate nation, the Union was also able to acquire debt through international borrowing, and trade continued to thrive. Lastly, the Union was able to continue to accept contributions from private investors and various taxes, since the wealthy business owners were able to maintain a profitable state of operation. Every plan the Confederacy had failed to realize, the Union had successfully employed with great success.

When the South was winning the war in the early years, there was not much inflation – as they say, to the victor go the spoils. As time dragged on and their economy weakened when Northern resolve did not seem to sway, however, the Confederacy was left with little choice. Facing defeat and tempted in the absence of another solution, it began printing money. From February, 1862 through February, 1864, the South experienced inflation that eventually reached over 700% per year [20]. A sharp decline in inflation was realized in March, 1864, after the Confederate government finally adopted monetary policy which reduced their supply of money by 67%. Unfortunately, this was a short lived victory, since the war effort was no longer fruitful and confidence in Confederate currency had been almost entirely washed away. By the end of the war in 1865, the cost of living in the South was 92 times what it had been at the start of the war, almost all of which can be attributed to poor monetary policies and a lack of confidence in Confederate money. Confederate money was so abundant that even today it carries little historical value.

Panic of 1907

Confidence in currency is probably the most important aspect of any currency. Without confidence in a currency's ability to store value and conduct trade, other markets – black markets, barter markets, alternative currency markets, etc. – may emerge where the legal tender is simply not utilized. We have witnessed a loss of confidence in markets and money many times throughout human history. We usually refer to the ebbs and flows of market forces or crashes and booms as the business cycle and it is not new.

The Panic of 1907 was not the first panic and it certainly was not the last. It is often thought-that the business cycle can be mitigated through fiscal or monetary intervention, and, in fact, much of the economics and banking professions are motivated by just such a thought. Given the number of recessions before and during the 19th century in the absence of a central bank, and the frequency of booms and busts in the 20th century in the presence of one, such an idea seems untenable. However, this does not mean we should not still try, nor does it mean we cannot learn from these cycles and legislate around such an abundance of empirical data. Furthermore, some of the ebbs and flows that have been caused by market panic or irrational exuberance could have been avoided if a central banking authority had existed. Counter-cyclical policy in fact reduced the effects of many of the recessions following the Great Depression.

Initial Symptoms for The Panic of 1907 were becoming evident when over-zealous prospectors attempted to corner the market for copper. In 1907, the industrialists Charles W. Morse, and Otto and Augustus Heinze began pooling investors to acquire as much stock as they could in the corporation United Copper. Large corporations such as the Knickerbocker Trust Company had contributed heavily to the effort. When the attempt, later deemed the Heinze-Morse scheme, to dominate the copper market failed, depositors in the major financial companies involved began demanding their deposits be returned out of fear the banks were on the verge of failure. On Friday, October 17th, 1907, a bank-run on The Knickerbocker was well underway and the Panic of 1907 would soon begin.

The Knickerbocker was a large financial institution which worked closely with many of the other financial entities in the New York area. Since many banks within New York were so tightly connected, it appeared that all financial institutions could be in trouble. Further troubling the markets was the lack of will to assist the larger institutions from failing when runs began to spread. Trust companies' presidents did not feel it was their responsibility to help, and the lenders of last resort of the day, various clearing houses such as the New York Clearing House, had reached their limits. The only hope was that the U.S. Treasury would step in to assist, but even the $25 million they loaned to various financial institutions did not prove large enough to quell the panic.

J.P. Morgan frantically organized bankers and trust presidents and using his personal credibility, managed to raise enough money to keep several banks solvent for a few days. The magnitude of the runs, however, did not decline and the private markets were unable to adapt. Even deposits from J. D. Rockefeller, in the amount of $10 million and promises of up to $40 million more if needed, did not stop the panic. There had been roughly ten economic panics since the 1850's, but this one was different, deeper, and was becoming more widespread.

Making problems worse, an earthquake had ravaged California and much of San Francisco had burned in a fire the previous year. There was so much damage that insurance companies were struggling to pay claims, and the demand for their deposits from various banks around the world was putting upward pressure on interest rates and pushing the United States toward recession. As the number of claims continued to rise, insurance companies began filing for bankruptcy or simply refusing to pay new claims, and the public at large was quickly losing faith in the entire financial system. The public distrust led to further runs on banks and demand for deposits continued to grow. Since money was directly exchangeable for gold, and in light of the emerging problems, many depositors had lost faith in the paper currency; the demand for gold in place of cash was rising [1].

As bankers attempted to comfort the public and eliminate the new distrust, their stocks of gold fell, and the stock market itself began displaying the panic the market was feeling. Like a self-fulfilling prophesy, the activity of the stock market further fueled the flames and the panic grew as the interest rate of call-money (money loaned that can be requested at a moment's notice, on-demand; it is not a term loan) rose from 6% to 100% in a single day, stopped only by the efforts of J. P. Morgan himself. The panic had caused many trust companies to recall their loans in an effort to remain solvent if bank runs continued to spread. Many banks and trusts even suspended operations as a result of the growing crisis. This in turn tightened the money supply in the markets and stock prices plunged. A temporary reprieve near the end of trading that day would prove unfruitful when similar demands on the market appeared the next day as well and call-money interest rates increased even further, topping 150%.

In the absence of a central bank, clearing houses served the purpose of lender of last resort. During previous crises they sometimes issued clearing house certificates that banks could trade among themselves, thus eliminating the trade of gold or cash and freeing up that money for demand deposits. In 1907, however, these certificates were delayed for fear it would further scare the public and deepen the crisis. Stronger banks could refuse to accept them, thus destroying rivals, and the public interest might give way to private interest [1]. The decision was finally made to allow the trade of certificates among banks in order to assist with bank liquidity. The certificates quelled market problems in the short term, but other problems were still brewing and the crisis was not localized to New York, or even the United States. In fact, money markets all over the world were facing pressures created by an outflow of gold from abroad and into the United States to meet liquidity demands. Further fanning the flames, New York City was virtually bankrupt and unable to acquire loans until J. P. Morgan stepped in with a loan from his own banking institutions.

The divestment of funds from all over the nation – and gold from all over the world – degraded economic confidence. Global financial instability, grouped with market conditions induced by the Heinze-Morse scheme in New York and the earthquake and subsequent San Francisco fire in 1906, the Panic of 1907 had begun through what seemed to be a perfect economic storm. Though many clearing houses existed at the time, none were wealthy or powerful enough to stop the panic that ensued in the face of such a dire liquidity crisis. The panic did not end until the markets had calmed and J. P. Morgan was able to organize some very large business deals that would have violated anti-trust laws without the expressed permission of President Theodore Roosevelt. Bank liquidity was restored, and the panic finally ended in 1908, but not before elucidating the need for some new form of centralized monetary authority that could mitigate future panics.

Creation of the Fed

Though the markets had calmed after the Panic of 1907, it was clear the entire system had to be rebuilt with more stability. There had been far too many panics in the century leading up to 1907, and their depth and severity seemed to be getting worse;

allowing the markets to self-calibrate no longer seemed viable. The clearing houses of the day had played a major role in keeping liquidity in the system throughout the many panics leading up to 1907, but they too teetered on the brink of failure during the crises [1]. Even the U.S. Treasury, which was dependent on tax income struggled to help when it seemed necessary.[4] Everyone involved in banking and industry knew a larger, more comprehensive entity must be created to stand ready to intervene when such crises emerged in the future.

A group of powerful, eager, and interested bankers and industrialists gathered in secret at Jekyll Island, Georgia at a conference in late November, 1910. Representatives attended on behalf of J.P. Morgan, John D. Rockefeller, and Kuhn, Loeb and Co. Those in attendance included a senator named Nelson W. Aldrich, Assistant Secretary of the U.S. Treasury Department, A. Piatt Andrew, and several powerful bankers of the day including Frank Vanderlip, Henry P. Davison, Charles D. Norton, Benjamin Strong, and Paul Warburg [21]. They determined the panics that had been growing in severity and capped by the panic of 1907 (actually the most severe occurred in 1893, but the uncertainty it created added to the Panic of 1907) were caused by an inelastic money supply and an overly complicated reserve system that hindered banks' ability to make loans [22].

On December 23, 1913, the Federal Reserve Act passed congress and was signed into law by President Woodrow Wilson. The organization that emerged was called the Federal Reserve System of the United States (Fed). This organization is both publicly and privately owned; its leadership is appointed by the

---

[4] At the time, the U.S. Treasury often had less money than the large corporations of the day. J.D. Rockefeller, for example, had more money on hand than the U.S. government.

President of the United States and confirmed by the United States Senate. Any money the Fed earns throughout the year is remitted to the United States Treasury and the Fed receives no funding from the federal government. The Federal Reserve is the only organization related to the federal government that is profitable every single year [23]. It contributes to the U.S. Treasury regularly, even in the wake of deregulation and the Great Recession of 2008.

When panics such as the Panic of 1907 occur, it is the job of the Fed to be the "lender of last resort." When liquidity begins to dry up in markets, like in 1907, the Fed can step in and lend to banks when other banks are unwilling or unable; the Fed can loosen the money supply to get funds flowing during frozen or very sluggish market conditions. The Federal Reserve was created in 1913 to solve precisely the problems that caused the Panic of 1907, and as new problems have come to light, the Fed has adapted to meet new challenges.

The Fed is allowed to create money on demand (from thin air essentially) and is entirely in charge of the United States monetary policy and money supply. Today the Fed's job is not easy since it has two mandates that are often at odds with one another. It is the job of the Fed to keep unemployment near its natural rate while also keeping inflation low, positive, and stable. To that end there are three main monetary tools the Fed uses to accomplish its two mandates. The Fed can change the reserve requirements of private Fed member banks, perform open market operations (a power not added until the 1930's), and change the discount rate member banks pay to borrow directly from the Fed. The Fed does not directly change market interest rates as is commonly misunderstood, but it does have great influence over them. Through open market operations and increases to the money supply the Fed can increase the quantity of money banks have in reserve, thereby indirectly influencing interest rates lower. As the supply of loanable funds[5] grows, the banks themselves decrease interest rates in order to encourage more borrowing. Just like how the prices of consumer goods may change the quantity demanded of those goods, the price of loanable funds – the interest rates – affects the quantity demanded of loanable funds.

A fear of the Fed, or a desire to return to the gold-standard, are understandable concerns from people who are worried about so much power held by a single entity. Understanding the mandate of the Fed should eliminate those concerns, however. By limiting the money in circulation, the Fed can keep the value of the dollar stable just like the naturally limited supply of gold keeps the value of gold stable. The Fed can adopt restrictive or contractionary policies and increase the value of the dollar, just like the value of gold increases in value when mines stop producing. The Fed can also adopt expansionary policies when liquidity in the system begins to seize. Expansionary policies are unique to a central bank like the Fed and can be used to boost aggregate demand and mitigate the depth of recessions; this is a power that is impossible with a true gold-standard.

The United States began its existence in debt and with a horrible amount of inflation [5]. Without a central bank to regulate the quantity of currency in circulation, the central government funded the Revolutionary War effort with the creation of currency known as "Continental Currency." Without any check on the system like a central bank, the money rapidly lost value as Congress ordered more and more of it to finance the war effort;

---

[5] Loanable funds are funds available to be loaned by banks to the general public, corporations, etc.

by the end of the war Continental Currency was practically worthless. The loss in value led to American's coining the phrase, "not worth a continental." The opposite was true of the Panic of 1907, which was a crisis in liquidity. In the absence of a central bank and the presence of a gold-backed currency, there was not enough money available to meet the demand for money as it increased and banks began going bankrupt. There are those who argue that the Fed has created a much more frequent, more volatile boom and bust cycle. However, the boom and bust cycle existed long before the creation of the Fed, and the problems the Fed was designed to solve, including the business cycle, have at least now become less severe. It is clear that without the Fed things could be much worse.

Importance of the Federal Reserve System

There were two U.S. central banks chartered before the Federal Reserve Bank of the United States. The second of those banks' charters expired in 1834, although the bank itself did not fail until 1841. President Andrew Jackson was disapproving of the central bank's existence and began pulling federal funds out of the bank in 1832. Following the federal government pulling more than 65% of its deposits, the bank struggled to survive even as a state chartered bank. It is estimated that the money supply grew drastically with an annual growth rate of nearly 30% between 1834 and 1836 after the federal charter ran out. The monetary growth rate had only averaged a reasonable 2.7% in the presence of the central bank [22].

The growth rate of money is important because it relates directly to inflation. When more money is created a shift in demand occurs as consumers begin buying more than they would have otherwise purchased. When demand rises producers see an opportunity to increase profit margins and will increase prices. In normal times, under monetary conditions with an average growth rate of only a few percentage points per year, this would not be problematic. However, when there are large swings in the money supply or when the supply of money is whimsical, uncertainty is created in the market. Uncertainty can drive market activity in very dangerous directions.

Uncertainty was at the center of the troubles that occurred during the Weimar Republic in Germany following World War I. Uncertainty helped drive the Soviet Union into its crisis in 1991, and more recently (2008) uncertainty drove Zimbabwe even further down the path of economic ruin. All three of these nations had one thing in common: a central bank that was not independent of the central government. When the government wanted to spend, it simply printed more money. When foreign nations demanded debt be repaid that was no problem either, they would just create more money to fill the need as it arose. When the people of these nations were too poor to make ends meet, the government's solution was to give them more money. It is not hard to win an election when one can promise wealth and riches to all of one's constituents, and that is exactly what the politicians of these nations did.

With a central bank that was tied to the central government, the Weimar Republic of Germany saw more than a 100 billion percent increase in prices in just four years. As Germany struggled to pay its bills following the treaty of Versailles, the German government commissioned the printing of more and more money. At one point there were over 200 factories producing paper just to keep up with the government's insatiable need to print more money. That means human and physical resources that could have been producing useful goods and activity that could drive and grow their economy in the longer term, were instead creating paper that had almost no value. In 1919 it cost only one mark for a loaf of bread, by 1923 its cost was over 100 billion marks [24].

In the early days of the Soviet Union, the Bolsheviks had trouble establishing an effective and stable monetary policy. Throughout the early period of the nation, the government had to redenominate[6] its currency on three separate occasions. As hyperinflation took hold and poor monetary policy continued, The three separate redenominations resulted in 50 billion old rubles being equal to one new ruble [25]. After the fall of the Soviet Union in 1991, the country was faced with another economic crisis and a very similar decision had to be made. From 1992 to 1998 the ruble devalued by roughly 4000%. Another redenomination occurred and one new ruble was trading for 1000 old rubles once again. Even after the redenomination the Russian government continued to devalue by another 25-35% in the same year before they finally stabilized their currency.

In 2006 Zimbabwe faced a similar economic crisis when it began printing large denomination bills to pay off foreign debts. The first of these payments occurred to the International Monetary Fund when the Zimbabwe central bank printed a Z$1 trillion bill for the payment. Since that period inflation has reared its ugly head to the tune of nearly 90 sextillion percent. That is a number most of us have never even heard of, so here is what it means. We think in terms of millions, then billions, and maybe trillions – possibly quadrillions assuming we are discussing

---

[6] Redenominating currency is when a nation changes the nominal value of money by exchanging older currency with one value for newer currency with a different value. Essentially they chop off zeroes from the hyper-inflated bills and renaming the money

astronomically large distances in space. But few consider that after quadrillion is quintillion and *then* sextillion. To give you a comparison, 1 trillion looks like this: 1,000,000,000,000. 1 sextillion looks like this: 1,000,000,000,000,000,000,000. Just for one more comparison that might make this make more sense to you, it has been estimated that there are about 700 quintillion grains of sand on earth. That looks like this: 700,000,000,000,000,000,000. So, this one bill in Zimbabwe in 2008 represented a figure that was more than 90 times the number of grains of sand on the entire earth, deserts and beaches included. Perhaps I do not need to say this, but Zimbabwe no longer has its own currency. Instead, they now utilize other nations' currencies for trade.

Governments and politicians often hope to get out of debt through the printing of new money or through the forgiveness of debts they owe. Even our most conservative politicians in the United States sometimes offer similar solutions. Ron Paul, former congressman from Texas, previous presidential candidate, and avid enemy of the Federal Reserve System, once stated that the government could avoid raising the public debt limit by simply not paying the Federal Reserve Bank what it was owed. It is true that the United States Government owes the Fed around $1.5-2 trillion, and several more trillion to other intragovernmental[7] agencies. However, it is a terrible idea to default on that debt simply because it is *"owed to ourselves,"* to use the words of Dr. Paul. As you can see from my previous examples, defaulting on intragovernmental debt is tantamount to government funding itself with its printing presses; it is the beginning of a very slippery slope and is precisely why our central bank (officially) has very limited ties to our government

---

[7] Intragovernmental lending is lending between agencies within the same government.

and politicians. Another solution to the U.S. debt crisis that has been considered by the treasury secretary (although probably not seriously considered) is that of minting a $1 trillion dollar coin to back our money. This is not an original idea and we can observe other nations in the world, such as Zimbabwe, to learn very quickly why this is certainly a very bad idea.

Allowing any government to have direct control over monetary policy is disastrous, ineffective, and counter-productive. Politicians may wish to wage wars or grow social programs, but they may choose to print money to pay for these choices instead of taxing. The people may hope for more riches and wealth, and politicians hoping to get elected may promise just that and then actually deliver, only to the chagrin of the entire economy. The nation may attempt to pay down debts, eliminate poverty, increase social programs, or pay for war, but it will only find new and deeper problems that it did not face before. It is not only good that we have a central bank, it is essential that that organization remains mostly outside the purview of politicians and absent the uncertainty of political whims. Thus the Federal Reserve Bank of the United States is essential to our economic stability, monetary strength, and its structure must remain unadulterated.

WWI, The Great Depression, and WWII

Contrary to popular belief, war is not good for anyone's economy. I am certain there will be economists who disagree with this perspective, and probably people and pundits as well, but I stand by the statement. A nation may employ its people in the military and industry may begin to thrive while producing military equipment, but the equipment produced only creates destruction and destroys wealth. Unemployment may decline but only because people are in the military instead of the workforce. The capital used to create military equipment may be more fully employed to produce weapons but only at the opportunity cost of more economically productive capital or consumer goods. The country who wins may see a boost to their economy, especially if they pillage the other nation, but overall the world economy as a whole will suffer from misused, lost, or unproductive wealth. Plus, war costs money and governments have to find financing for the enterprise at the expense of social programs and infrastructure development.

The traditional economic example used to justify how war might be good for an economy is the story of the broken window. When a window is broken then the window repair person has a job. The window manufacturer employs window makers and those who collect raw natural materials now also have gainful employment. When the window is repaired the money flows from the owner of the original window through the supply chain and everyone has new income. The money is spent more than once and we see a multiplicative effect on the economy overall, therefore we logically conclude that more people are employed, manufacturing is healthy, and the economy is growing. Unfortunately this is not the full story. If the owner of the broken window had never had a broken window in the first place then he could have used the money for some other purpose. The owner's alternative purchase could have contributed exactly the same effect on the economy while improving his own standard of living simultaneously without the loss of the value of the window.

The major difference can be observed in the value of the window before and after it is broken. If the window remained unbroken then the owner of the window would be able to spend his money on other consumer or productive goods. The economy would still get the multiplicative effect plus the value of the unbroken window would not be lost. When the window becomes broken the economy loses the original value of the window before any other activity occurs. The multiplier effect is only realized after the repair but it will be smaller since we must subtract the value of the broken window from any other economic gain – in other words, wealth is destroyed. The owner of the original window cannot purchase other consumer or productive goods but instead has to pay for the repair of the broken window. Therefore the owner of the window is left with a lower standard of living as a result. Similarly, war is not good for the economy. Though production and manufacturing increase, it is only through the destruction of wealth that demand for new goods is created.

Wartime manufacturing thrived in the early years of WWI and the German economy was soaring. However, as the war progressed and scarce resources were used for the production of wartime goods instead of food and consumer manufacturing, the German economy waned. Money became less valuable as the government printed more and more to cover wartime costs. War bonds were difficult to exchange as the government paid them off with money that was quickly losing its value. The war effort was weakening in the presence of poor morale created by the struggling economy, and two out of every three soldiers either deserted or refused to return to the front after a furlough. It was not until after the war, however, that the real economic hardships began. To pay for wartime debts and unreasonable demands forced on them by the Treaty of Versailles, the government of Germany simply printed even more money when payments to the allies became difficult. Eventually the money held no value at all. When manufacturing moved to the production of paper for money instead of economically productive goods, the economy suffered even further. Instead of producing growth through production, sale, and hopefully exportation of goods and services, productive capacity was converted, and subsequently wasted, to print worthless monetary notes. Germany's poor economic position did not improve; in fact, it was degrading [24].

Even as Germany struggled, the U.S. economy was roaring through the 1920s. Economist Murray N. Rothbard estimated that the U.S. money supply grew by over 60% between 1921 and 1928 – a loose monetary policy that would certainly increase aggregate demand and a boom in the U.S. economy [26]. Averaging nearly a 7% increase in the supply of money per year, immense economic activity and growth throughout the 1920's spurred aggregate demand. In 1929, however, things took a turn for the worst. When the Federal Reserve began fearing inflation caused by the ever increasing supply of money, they adopted a contractionary monetary policy, and most likely triggered the stock market crash of 1929. Further contractionary monetary policy caused another crash in 1931 and continued poor monetary policy prolonged the great depression. It was not until Nov 7th, 1941 that the economy would get a reprieve when the United States entered WWII.

WWII did not cause the U.S. or world economy to improve, but it certainly took the unemployed out of the workforce and helped reduce the unemployment rate. During the war, manufacturing of military goods increased and civilian manufacturing decreased. Food was rationed and though a spirit of patriotism was born, the standard of living all over the world was reduced. War funding was acquired through borrowing, and perhaps the largest body of proof for the effectiveness of fiscal spending was created.

Keynesian economists and politicians argued that the war increased manufacturing and improved the productive capability of the nation. They feared that when the war ended there would be a large recession do to the decrease in wartime spending. When the recession did not come as predicted, however, the Keynesian believers cried foul. The end of the war did not spell disaster to Hayekian (Free market, non-interventionist) economists, however; it meant a new beginning. Ending the war meant an end to fiscally irresponsible spending and a conclusion of artificial growth. The Great Depression had ended, the war was over, and soldiers returning home could once again undertake economically productive activity. New entrepreneurs could begin new businesses and the free market could function naturally once again.

As is so often the case, both Hayekians and Keynesian believers were correct with their predictions simultaneously. Rarely do economists consider that both Hayek and Keynes could be correct at the same time, especially from their very different perspectives. The fiscal cost of the war meant the government had placed hundreds of millions of dollars into the hands of returning soldiers. Though the government had to either borrow or tax to pay for the expense, there is no doubt that the money spent by the government produced economic growth after the war. Keynesians had nothing to fear from an end to government spending on the war itself, since the soldiers coming home would spend the money they had saved while fighting. Therefore government spending unquestionably paved the way for private investment and economic growth. Hayekians also had nothing to fear from the government spending on military equipment during the war. The soldiers themselves would self-organize and invest their savings when they returned from the front and the free market would function as expected.

Government spending had funded investment – as Keynesians had predicted, just not through the method they had originally considered. Government spending had created economic activity – not through central planning as Hayekians had feared, but through plans by the many as Hayekians had desired.

I do not mean to make the case that the Second World War was good for the U.S. economy, but it did allow the government to spend and provided certain people no other choice except to save. During the war military manufacturing increased and productive capability grew inside the United States; the economy grew. After the war civilians invested in entrepreneurial activity and took over the manufacturing infrastructure the government had utilized during the war; the economy grew yet further. The war itself was unnecessary if economic growth was the objective, however. The government could easily have adopted a helicopter policy, namely by estimating the cost of something as expensive as the Second World War, borrowing that amount, and mailing a check to every American for a portion of the funds. Strangely enough, that sort of policy would likely cause uncertainty and inflation while truly harming the economy.

Finally, the war is not what truly created the economic position the U.S. found itself in after its conclusion. Although there were certainly positive economic impacts following the soldiers returning home and from the wartime spending and saving, they were not universal to the entire world. Europe was in ruins, Asia was rebuilding, and people were suffering from South America all the way through Africa and into the Pacific Rim by proxy connections to their economies. Imports and exports were slowed across the globe during the war and the world economy was in shambles. The U.S. was only able to step up as the world economic power because of the Marshal Plan and the Bretton-Woods agreement.

Bretton Woods and Leaving the Gold-Standard

In the midst of World War II, several world leaders gathered at Bretton Woods, NH, to discuss the rebuilding of the world economy. They knew waiting until after the war concluded to address such concerns could exhaust enthusiasm for the effort and possibly result in circumstances much like those after World War I. It was clear the war would not last much longer and that rebuilding the world would be a complicated and expensive undertaking. Without an international agreement, nations would likely devalue their currencies, compete for exports, argue over war debts, and possibly drive the world back into dismay, much like after World War I.

Since the world's most powerful industrial centers had been greatly impacted by the war, and since infrastructure in many nations was badly damaged, rebuilding the world's economy after the Great War seemed to be an insurmountable undertaking. Most of the nations who had been involved in the war effort were essentially broke and needed capital investment before they could even consider resuming production or trade. The Bretton Woods agreement was signed to address these problems specifically.

In order to rebuild their economies, participating nations agreed that a system of international trade needed to be established and that a common currency for trade would be needed.[8] The International Monetary Fund (IMF) was created to regulate trade

---

[8] Keynes hoped for a new currency called the "bancor,", but the dollar was chosen to his dismay.

imbalances, exchange rates of member nations, and fill liquidity gaps as they emerged. The International Bank for Reconstruction and Development (today known as the World Bank) was created to facilitate loans, underwrite private loans, and to encourage faster growth for nations emerging from the second world-war.

Member nations would leave the gold-standard, with the exception of the United States, and accept dollars as the world reserve currency. Dollars would still be convertible at a ratio of $35 to every one ounce of gold indefinitely. International exchange rates needed to maintain some stability; thus, every nation in the world agreed to tie the value of their currency to the U.S. Dollar, and the Dollar attained world reserve currency status. Before any nation would be allowed to change the value of its currency by more than 10% it would first have to get approval from the international community – specifically the IMF, which was directly influenced by the U.S. government.

As one might imagine, the reserve currency status of the dollar provided unbalanced economic power to the United States who could adopt a fractional gold-reserves system and loan more money to the world than it actually had on deposit. Furthermore, since exchange rates were tied to the dollar, American consumers could import more foreign-made goods, thus benefitting American consumers, domestic importers, and foreign exporters. The improved status of the dollar made Americans wealthier and enabled foreign nations to acquire much needed financial capital to invest in their infrastructures and economies. Foreign nations were happy to be exporting. U.S. corporations also benefited as they were able to invest in capital goods abroad, a welcomed action for any nation who was getting an influx of productive capacity. As dollars were spent abroad, the balance of trade for the U.S. widened, and large trade deficits were incurred. The Fed largely ignored the net outflow of U.S. dollars since the exchange rates were locked, and instead focused on domestic monetary policy, as mandated. The outflow, however, put inflationary pressure on foreign made goods and the dollar lost value in terms of tradable goods – but not in terms of gold.

As the dollar became less valuable abroad, the value of gold should have increased. However, the Bretton Woods agreement had the exchange rate of gold tied to the dollar and the U.S. government did not have the power to unilaterally change the value of convertibility. To further exacerbate the problem, several nations began buying gold from the United States and selling it to speculators in a secondary market at a profit. By 1967 the U.S. refused to sell gold to nations who sold to private investors, but the damage was already done. In 1968 the London Gold Pool (the nations who had contributed to the supply of gold to maintain Bretton Woods) began to collapse when France demanded its deposits be returned so it could escape the coming collapse. Since the dollar had been devalued through the excess American spending abroad, it was becoming more evident that it was no longer directly convertible to gold. Bretton Woods was no longer viable.

In 1971 The United States left the gold-standard. As dollars began to flow back to the Treasury, demanding gold in exchange, gold reserves fell and the U.S. approached the verge of bankruptcy. The final straw occurred when the U.S. government learned that Great Britain was about to claim its dollar equivalent of gold deposits from the U.S. Treasury. Since the United States only had about 1/3 of those deposits on hand, the claim would have been tantamount to a run on the U.S.

Treasury, and would have bankrupted the country. Seeing this was a very likely outcome, and only weeks before it was going to occur, on August 15, 1971, President Richard Nixon announced the United States was temporarily leaving the gold-standard. The temporary pause to the exchange of dollars into gold halted the international bank-run, and protected the nation's economy.

The Bretton Woods agreement had tied the hands of U.S. monetary policy and held the value of U.S. money at a higher level than it would have been if the dollar had been a floating currency. Had the value of the dollar been allowed to float against gold, the gold-standard might well be in effect today. It should be noted, however, that even today the U.S. dollar is a safe investment and remains the world's reserve currency. The Federal Reserve has maintained the stability of the dollar, and many nations still peg their currencies to the dollar. Nations deposit dollars in their treasuries and back their own currencies as if the dollar is as sound as it ever has been. The dollar is still used for international loans and aid, and is still the common measuring rod for important commodities such as oil. One departing thought: the U.S. has never returned from the temporary suspension of the gold-standard that President Nixon announced.

Gold Is Also Arbitrary

Currency is only as valuable as the faith those that use it have in its value. Any currency can be valuable; even sand could be currency if everyone in one's community utilized it for trade and had faith in its value. So those that argue gold is the only true money, with the only true value, do so from more of a sentimentally, historical position and on no real logical grounds.

Even Adam Smith knew gold was no more valuable than any other means of trade when he stated, *"Labour was the first price, the original purchase – money that was paid for all things. It was not by gold or by silver, but by labour, that all wealth of the world was originally purchased."*

Gold, just like dollars, is valuable because we assign it value based on the rarity of its existence and the labor needed for its extraction. Karl Marx wrote, *"In the use-value of each commodity there is contained useful labour, i.e., productive activity of a definite kind and exercised with a definite aim."* If we utilize useful labor to produce useless items for trade, then those useless items must represent at least the value of the labor used to produce them; therefore, we assign value to gold.

To drive this point home, consider diamonds and pennies. The penny has relatively no value; even that which it is assigned has almost no purchasing power. Perhaps because of its face value, or maybe because of the number of pennies in circulation, people drop, ignore, donate, or forget their pennies. They would never do this with diamonds, however. A gem quality diamond can be as small as 0.01 carats and reach a value of $10 each. According to the U.S. Mint, there are about 6.9 billion pennies in circulation and according to Bain & Company, there are roughly 133 million carats of diamonds mined each year. If we simplify diamonds to a universal size, quality, and weight, we can create about 13.3 billion 0.01 carat gem quality diamonds each year. In other words, there are more 0.01 carat gem quality diamonds in the world than pennies in circulation, yet we assign thousands of dollars of value to diamonds and almost no value to pennies [27] [28].

Gold is the same, although far more limited in quantity. We assign gold value because it has always had value – a circular argument to be sure – or, going further back through history, we could claim it has value because of the labor necessary to extract it from the earth. Short of its use in electronics or jewelry, and given its limited quantity, gold, like diamonds, has no real value other than that placed on it through the faith of those who prefer it and the labor of those who produced it. Through its use value, or the marginal utility acquired from its exchange, gold may have value, or it may have value due to the labor needed for its extraction. However, as long as gold is just sitting in a vault, it has no more value than the sand on the beach.

Furthermore, faith in gold is much like faith in fiat currency. It is backed by the full faith and credit of those who assign it value, just like money is backed by the full faith and credit of the United States government. The government promises you will acquire a dollar's worth of goods and services for each dollar you exchange. However, the government can default on that promise. Similarly, the claim is that if money was backed by gold then it would be exchangeable from the government directly for gold and the government could not default. However, that claim also means one must have faith that the government will provide the equivalent amount of gold for the value of a dollar, and there is no guarantee that the government will honor that obligation. In fact, in 1971 it was proven just how easy it is for government to default on such an obligation. Just as fiat currency is backed by the full faith and credit of the U.S. government, a gold backed currency is backed by the full faith and credit that the U.S. government will fulfill its promise of exchange from currency into gold. That promise is no more valuable for gold than it is for dollars.

We must always remember world history. Before the Bretton Woods agreement was suspended in 1971, the U.S. government – like other governments throughout history – utilized a fractional reserve, gold-backed currency. Therefore, the government may simply not be able to exchange currency for gold since it may have loaned more than it actually has on reserve. Refusing to exchange fiat currency for gold is not unprecedented, since the government did essentially default on its promise to exchange money for gold when it suspended the Bretton Woods agreement.

Another problem gold has is that it is an inconvenient way to conduct transactions. It is heavy, bulky, dirty, and there is not enough in the world for it to be utilized as currency. Creating a gold-note for conducting business, easing trade, and paying debts, is no more secure than backing our currency via a central bank and fiat currency. Backing our currency with gold is just as arbitrary as backing our money with fairy dust. Filling a vault with gold and stating that the value of gold is x dollars is equally as pointless as it sitting, useless, in that same vault.

Allowing the value of gold to float against the quantity of currency in circulation already occurs and is more effective than an arbitrary gold/dollar exchange rate. No central authority, no public agreement, and no reasons exist to go back to a government controlled gold-standard. It is not difficult to find a gold dealer in most cities. The value of gold floats with the dollar, so the dollar value of gold changes as the value of the dollar changes. On any given day anyone can look up the price of gold and see that it fluctuates regularly. The supply and demand for gold changes its value, and so does the supply and demand for the U.S. dollar. Just like any other good or service produced, if the value of the dollar drops, the price of that good will be higher. If the value of the dollar improves, the price of goods will be less. Again, the perceived benefits of gold money, or a gold-backed currency, are outweighed by the problems gold has introduced in the past. The problems it would create in our present and future are difficult to gauge, but they would likely be even more complex when combined with the electronic and fiat exchange of the 21st century.

Chapter 3: Politics and Economics

"… the prince may either spend his own wealth or that of his subjects, or the wealth of others; in the first case he must be frugal; in the second, he must not omit any aspect of liberality."
Nicolò Machiavelli

Projecting the Future

It is the job of economists to look to the past, act in the present, and plan for the future. Utilizing the skills they have acquired through years of training and experience, they are expected to research and project where our economy will go based on where it is and where it has been before. Furthermore, they are expected to investigate policies to create greater growth and higher standards of living. I have discussed growth in our economy, the expectation of continued growth, and its importance at length with my brother on many occasions. It is his contention that growth is not only unnecessary, but that it is wasteful. Why, he asks, is it necessary to continue to grow the economy when we have everything we need right now, live comfortably, and retain healthy, happy lives? I will answer this question by first looking into the past.

It may seem strange to consider, but kings during the middle ages had worse living conditions than the most impoverished American does today – assuming they are not homeless. Most Americans eat out on a regular basis; thus, they have cooks, servers, and butlers to clean up — akin to royalty having servants in the past. Perhaps we do not consider that we have assistance getting dressed each day, but we use a machine to clean our clothes, a water heater to warm our shower, and a fan to cool our bedroom. Maybe we think kings had it better because they were kings, but rarely did they have running water or clean toilets; they certainly never had air-conditioning. These are only a few of the improvements we enjoy, but how many others have I ignored? We take our standard of living for granted and ignore all the amenities that kings did not even enjoy – we are spoiled and do not even know it.

Does being spoiled mean we should not strive for further improvements in our standard of living? No, and only through growth can we achieve a higher standard of living. It seems absurd to consider living like peasants during the middle ages, but today there are over a billion people on earth living in exactly those conditions. This means one of every seven people on earth lives in abject poverty; that is nearly 15% of the entire world's population. Imagine the future, say 500 years from now; will people look back on our civilization with similar astonishment? Will there be a billion people living in America's current standard of living, but labeled as impoverished? If that is the world of the future, then by our current standards that is a huge success! To achieve that success, we must continually grow our economy. Growing our economy does not mean we cannot change our workweeks, working hours, or the amount of time we spend with our families, but it does mean we must grow. It does not mean we have to negatively impact our environment or destroy sensitive species, reefs, or arctic areas. It means we must be conscious of how we grow and mitigate the impact we have on the world and the environment where we live. Our current level of existence cannot continue indefinitely. Growth, for the first time in history, is required if we wish to maintain our existing standard of living. Oil reserves are being depleted, carbon dioxide levels in the atmosphere are building, water resources are becoming contaminated, ocean fisheries are being weakened, and soil nutrients are being sapped. Without growth, new technologies to address these very disturbing problems are unlikely to emerge, and our very way of life will remain threatened.

A growing economy does not only mean an improved standard of living and safety from destruction, but also an improved state of being. That improved state of being includes decreased working hours, shorter work weeks, more time with those we love, and a clean environment in which to live. Growth can lead to a labor/leisure decision that is more heavily focused on leisure. Leisure is the time we strive so hard to acquire through the fruits of our daily labor. It is the time we spend with our families and friends and the ability to pursue our personal interests. People should be proud of the leisure time they utilize; it should not be a source of shame. We must learn to ignore this shameful taboo that seems to have emerged in our culture.

To attain a sustainable and improved standard of living we must adopt policies for growth through effective advice to our leadership. To achieve that goal, we must adapt to our technology, our world, and our new level of comfort while continually seeking even greater improvements, technologies, and sustainability. To achieve a greater state of being, we must evolve to understand those who are less productive, accept that we can be personally less productive as we shift some of our efforts to the machines our great inventors have so earnestly created, and then more effectively enjoy the short time we are given. To grow we must avoid the ever-present ideological entrenchment where so many find themselves deeply mired.

Advising the Leadership

Earlier in this book I introduced a quote from Harry S Truman that epitomizes the problem with advice to leadership (*"Give me a one handed economist...*"). For every political or economic problem, solutions often create new problems. Working through these problems can be difficult, and that is why we hire economists to complete research and advise leadership on economic solutions. Economists have a tendency, however, to provide every side of the coin; after all, it is their job to think of every problem and contingency that possibly emerges. Even writing this paragraph I am finding it difficult to explain the two-handed economist, because every sentence creates two more sentences that each require two more sentences to explain! In a chaotic world where every problem has multiple solutions that each have their very own set of problems and another level of even more solutions, how is anyone to advise anyone else effectively?

Because of the divergent paths economists have to straddle, they must utilize gut feelings on a regular basis. Depending on which philosophy they adopt, they typically give advice which leans in that direction. Paul Krugman, for example, often advises very Keynesian policies while Glenn Hubbard pushes for more free market orientated policies. These two world-class economists almost always disagree, but one of them is often correct under certain market conditions while the other is correct under different conditions. They are philosophically opposed, but both nurture a world-class reputation and the power to match. Each advises different politicians and depending on which party retains a majority, each achieves a different level of persuasion over government policy.

Advising the leadership comes with its own set of problems, but those problems change depending on the state of the economy. Again, under some conditions Dr. Krugman is correct while Dr. Hubbard finds his answers lacking. Under other conditions Dr.

Hubbard finds he is absolutely justified in his positions while Dr. Krugman learns of his shortcomings. There is a third, often overlooked position in the west, where neither Paul Krugman nor Glenn Hubbard may provide the more accurate assessment. Under some circumstances neither Austrian nor Keynesian solutions find their way to a successful economic prescription.

Economic indicators elucidate the state of the economy and then a policy must be chosen to match those conditions. Economic forecasting is utilized to attack economic problems that emerge in the modern world. Still, projecting the future is just about impossible. In the words of Eugene Ionesco, *"You can only predict things after they have happened."* Depending on which economist one asks, a different solution is suggested and usually those solutions are influenced by philosophically entrenched positions. Though the policies and answers are always more complex, they essentially boil down to three possible outcomes:

1. Do nothing since the economy will self-regulate and redirect resources and activities via the invisible hand.
2. Intervene to influence the direction of the economy, typically by proxy laws, regulations, monetary and fiscal policies but not by direct means or government ownership.
3. Directly intervene and centrally plan the entire economic system, possibly including some level of government ownership over the means of production.

I have laid out three distinct possibilities for intervention, and wrapped them up with a neatly tied bow. However, it is important to mention that these are far more complex than how I have presented them above. There are various grades of each, different methods for their implementation, and conditions for which one, two, or all methods might prove appropriate. What I hope the reader will take from the simplicity of the explanation is that we should not rule out any solution, no matter how unpopular the idea may have become over the course of history. The reader must remember, nations, ethnic groups, and political parties (essentially anyone with an agenda or something to gain) will spend billions of dollars on propaganda to stigmatize ideas and opposition groups, be they political, economic, or otherwise, during times of great stress – like the Cold War.

The use of economic models can often lead to a better informed decision, no matter what ideology one prefers, but there is no substitute for experience and knowledge. No matter which economic models we employ there is always some uncertainty, not to mention that even the most complex economic models barely scratch the surface of the vast number of real-world variables. Since policy is often based on advice from economists who utilize models to make predictions, and those models are really only an informed guide at best, a philosophical perspective always sways the final advice. Unfortunately, some philosophical perspectives have found their way into obscurity or, worse, perceived lunacy, and are simply never even considered as viable options.

National Policy and Development

When the federal government of the United States invested over $500 million into Solyndra, a solar panel manufacturing company, the taxpayers had no idea the company would eventually go bankrupt and never repay over $400 million of the original loan. Free market economists, conservative pundits, and libertarian citizens alike were all discussing how government intervention into technology was not necessary and that the free market would create opportunities as they became profitable. Of course they all ignore that the free market only adopts profitable technologies and has very little incentive to research expensive, new inventions before they are the child of necessity. By that point, however, we could have reached a point of no return. Water resources could be irreparably damaged, air quality could be incredibly degraded, and climate change could become completely irreversible.

As long as existing solutions and inventions are profitable, corporations have little incentive to change how they operate; such is the nature of capitalism. Capitalism offers many great benefits, but it is not flawless and is coupled with many dangers as well. Without an existing economy of scale it becomes difficult to find incentives for new investment into the production of important new technologies like carbon capture, solar roadways, or electric cars. When corporations do not wish to change or innovate, they may even hinder advancement through lobbying efforts which can even mitigate the development of new technologies.

Short of the world running out of oil, or demand rising so high that the price of oil explodes, the free market may never invest in wind power, solar power, wave power, or other alternative sources of energy. Free market advocates – I should clarify that I count myself as a free market advocate under *most* conditions, but not all – often ignore that the Internet was created by the Department of Defense. They often ignore that discoveries in rocket propulsion, leading to jetliner technology, was funded by the federal government. They ignore that every college in the country funds research with government funds that lead to life-saving technologies such as cancer treatment, heart disease treatment, HIV treatment, etc. They ignore that the world's most prestigious and effective research organization on everything relating to health, the NIH, is funded directly by the federal government. They ignore that government investment is sometimes necessary.

I teach in my class that the world's most important innovation was that of the granary. Ten thousand years ago every human was a hunter-gatherer, but when the granary was invented it allowed for a sedentary civilization. This invention gave the people time to innovate and without it we all might still be cave-people. They used this time to innovate philosophy, literature, mathematics, and engineering, which all lead to more time people could spend on invention and further innovation. These, of course, were all free market interactions done for the good of the entire community, with little or no profit motive. Surely this invention led to the creation of government also, as villages emerged with common needs such as defense and private property protection.

As our civilization marched through history, we found ourselves encapsulated in a capitalist society where the time to innovate has increasingly been capitulated to that of our vocation; it was sacrificed for that of quick comfort instead of long term improvement. Will the free market push us to ever higher standards? Yes, but it will be a slow and arduous task. Common people often lack the necessary connections, skills, and resources to bring important inventions to market. They sometimes have inadequate income to invest in experimentation, research, trial and error, and a proper, efficient level of capital investment. Can government intervention, through grants, loans, and other forms of funding assist with new endeavors and overcome these problems? Yes, and it will be much faster than waiting on only a few corporations or wealthy researchers. Government can expand the scope of research from only a few to a great many with enormous economic impacts. This occurs right now through government investment into universities and think tanks, with considerable success.

Economists often argue that government intervention is not efficient. I agree with this sentiment but believe this inefficiency is only a short term loss. As time progresses, small gains to our new development level due to the initial government intervention and investment will propel us to far higher levels, justifying a short-term loss in favor of future gains. Private industry can do investment better and probably for less money. Private industry would likely do it more efficiently and with a better outcome. When private industry is not spending, however, the government can finance the necessary investment on behalf of the people without waiting decades for the investment to become attractive to private industry.

Solyndra turned out to be a failure of monumental proportion. However, that does not mean all large-scale government investment will fail. It was through government investment – not private – that the U.S. interstate system, a 20th century technology, was built. Although America's private industry still has not invested in high speed rail in the United States, it was through governmental investment that Europe, Japan, and China have built such high-speed railways. It is through government investment that China has become the world's largest producer of steel and one of the fastest growing economies. It is likely that only through government investment will the United States finally build the next generation of infrastructure, but only if the ideologically entrenched allow for an investment into our future economic growth potential.

Healthcare and the Single Payer System

The United States was at the forefront of welfare systems in the middle of the twentieth century, with the creation of the Social Security Administration, Medicare, and Medicaid. These programs ensured people would not fall into poverty or poor health when they became too old to work. These systems virtually ended abject poverty among those in their twilight years. Through their creation the average United States citizen saw their lifespan improve from an expectation of just less than 63 years in 1940 to almost 79 years in 2010. It is true that there are many other factors to consider, but access to healthcare, a reduction of stress related to poverty after retirement, and the assurance of food and affordable nutrition certainly contributed greatly.

Today there are more than thirty countries with some sort of universal healthcare system, and the United States is not one of them – unless you count the Affordable Care Act, which seems to be a poor substitute for the single payer system. (In a single payer system, the government pays our medical bills through the collection of taxes or fees instead of the free market mechanism.) Countries with universal healthcare are diverse and include some of the economically freest nations in the world, like Hong Kong and Singapore, as well as nations with somewhat less economic freedom, like Slovenia and Kuwait. Advanced nations like France and the United Kingdom all have universal healthcare and they get it without much increase to their tax burden when compared to the United States. However, the largest, most advanced economy in the world has, so far, been unable to pass the necessary legislation. There are many arguments for and against such a system, coming from both sides of the ideological divide, and some are more relevant than others.

Many question the efficacy of our system, but most believe it is a fair, free market solution. Most would be incorrect. The free market solution only works when prices are visible and consistent, and consumers have clear choices and the ability to substitute to improved or less expensive options. In the United States, consumers do not have that ability in healthcare; prices are not visible or consistent, and the free market does not truly function in healthcare. Doctors only compete by changing the quality of the care they provide, and even that is often difficult or impossible for the average consumer to measure and/or ascertain. Lastly, even the doctors who wish to provide the best care available are limited by the shortage of time they can spend with their patients.

The first major argument against the universal healthcare system in the United States is that it will simply cost the taxpayer too much money. This is a valid point when one asks how such a system would be funded. To understand the flaw in this argument, however, one must first explore the history of healthcare costs and insurance in the United States. By 1960, after a 20 year period when the number of private health insurance plans grew more than seven times in the United States, the nation spent only 5.0% of GDP on national health expenditures (compared to roughly 17% today). That spending equated to only $147 per person [29] – the equivalent of $1,128 in 2012. More than 70% of Americans actually had some form of health coverage at that time, and even the Kerr-Mills act did not expand coverage to many more [30]. By 2012 that number had only increased to about 85% [31], not nearly a large enough increase to justify a demand shift that would equate to a price increase of the magnitude we see today. The sad fact is that we actually spent $8,915 per person on healthcare related expenses in 2012 [29], more than 7 times what we spent in 1960 when only 15% fewer people had some form of health coverage.

The price for hospital care more than doubled between 1950-1960, absent Medicare or Medicaid, and continued to rise as new technologies were adopted, inflationary pressures expanded, and reform legislation continued to find resistance through the 1970s, 80s, and 90s [30]. Insurance companies complained of doctors exploiting the payment systems; direct marketing began to increase, and all medical costs rose even further through the 2000s. Costs have risen despite the illusion of private markets controlling healthcare. There are many causes to increased medical costs in the United States: lack of pricing transparency, increased demand, increasing incomes, new regulations, government intervention, and research costs is a short list of the many reasons prices may have risen since 1960. It is worth noting that medical cost in France, the U.K., and Canada (the common comparable countries when discussing healthcare in the United States), are less than the United States, even under their single-payer system. In fact, healthcare costs are greater in the United States than any other developed nation, including those with single payer systems [32].

We must question why the price of healthcare increased so much over that period, and the answer is not the Great Society reforms in the 1960s. Research and development has increased in capacity and ability; many large health insurance companies have formed; malpractice insurance has become popular and necessary among doctors concerned about the also popular and frivolous lawsuits; HMO and PPO contract pricing is common, and government regulations over healthcare are continually increasing. Perhaps most importantly consumers lost their ability to actually see the price of their healthcare. Customers in the United States do not benefit from competition among doctors since they are unable to see the price they are paying for their care. Patients are willing to do any test the doctor orders since the doctor bills insurance. When a consumer is not concerned by the cost of care, otherwise costly or possibly unnecessary tests are completed at the insurer's expense and at the chagrin to all who buy ever more expensive health insurance. Consumer decisions might change if they were directly paying the bill, and doctors might change their decisions on testing if they did not earn more for each test they run. Including such transparency in pricing and responsibility in payments is not how the system is run today; the free market has vanished in healthcare.

Furthermore, people are unable to call various doctors, surgeons, or hospitals to get the prices for particular procedures; insurance companies negotiate different prices and contracts for everyone, and health costs continue to rise. This encourages unfair pricing practices that consumers also cannot see. When a doctor gets paid different amounts of money from each insurer, or even different prices depending on the multitude of various insurance plans, few benefit and costs rise. In economics we typically call this price discrimination, the act of charging different customers different prices with the hope of moving as much consumer surplus over to the producer as possible. Usually we discuss it in the context of companies like airlines, but it is perhaps more prevalent among healthcare providers.

Price discrimination does not benefit doctors either. Since doctors are dependent on insurance negotiators and also do not have the market power to demand greater accountability or better payment schemes, they inevitably receive less compensation and are forced to see more patients than the free market would likely otherwise require. They might compensate through ordering extra tests or checking additional boxes during their exam. When I was in college I once had a doctor candidly explain that while I had insurance he would check every box they were allowed to bill to insurance, a cost of nearly $250 for a normal office visit. When I told him I no longer had insurance, he checked two boxes for a total cost of $60, yet I had received exactly the same exam.

The quality of healthcare has fallen below where we should accept or expect at this point in our history. Doctors are forced to see so many patients each day that they are limited to only a few minutes with each person. This lack of time with their patients has degraded their ability to diagnose many problems and has even contributed to the rise of antibiotic resistant strains of various bacteria. Without the time to properly swab, test, and diagnose the cause of a sore throat, for example, a doctor may simply prescribe antibiotics and send the patient home. This sort of over-reaction to simple ailments has degraded our ability to treat many illnesses since the bacteria or viruses evolve to resist known treatments.

When Alexander Fleming discovered penicillin in 1928, it was probably the greatest breakthrough in healthcare in human history. Overuse (or under-eradication) has unfortunately led to drug resistant strains of many bacteria and viruses. Even tuberculosis (TB), previously treatable and not terribly disconcerting in countries like the United States for several decades, has evolved into many different strains, some curable and some not. Of them there are three terrifying categories: multi-drug resistant, extensively drug resistant, and totally drug resistant. Even the wealthiest of countries are not immune to antibiotic resistant bugs.

The next major argument against the universal healthcare system in the United States is that our healthcare is superior and will be diluted if it is universal to all, free of charge. This argument is also not true. Treatments for major illnesses are sought in many countries, the United States among them, but many have excellent healthcare systems. Germany, for example, is among the best in the world. To get a good comparison for the quality of care across countries, we must utilize various measures. When comparing infant mortality or life expectancy at birth, for example, we find the United States is comparable with the other OECD countries[9], but not the best in both categories. Studies also report similar results when examining survival rates from various cancers. In fact, the U.S. is even the worst in some categories when compared to Australia, Canada, England, and New Zealand [33]. The World Health Organization did a study researching the health system efficiency of their 191 member states and reported that among their highest performing members, the United States fell into only the third highest category after Canada, Spain, France, Portugal, United Kingdom, and a large portion of the rest of Europe [34]. Even Saudi Arabia was ranked better.

Another major argument against the universal healthcare system in the United States is that it will cause a shortage of doctors and medical personnel. The argument, that by creating a single-payer system in this country medical personnel will find the cost of schooling too oppressive to justify their profession after training, is that a shortage of doctors and nurses will be realized. Increased wait times at emergency rooms or decreased access to

---

[9] The Organization for Economic Cooperation and Development (OECD) is an organization of the most advanced economies in the world, and they work to promote growth, prosperity, and sustainable development.

medical personnel will be dangerous to those in dire need. Unfortunately for those who are against such a system, once again, the evidence to support that claim is in short supply. The World Bank reports that in 2011 the United States had 2.5 doctors for every 1000 members of society compared to 2.8 per 1000 in United Kingdom, and 3.4 per 1000 in France. Wait times for elective surgery and to see specialists is shorter in The United States versus United Kingdom but times are nearly equivalent to France (where they have also managed to avoid waiting lists for specialists) [35]. Seeing a doctor on the same day also does not vary much between the United States, United Kingdom, or France. So the argument that waiting for care will take longer, or that there will not be enough doctors in this nation after implementing such a policy is entirely unconvincing.

As the system is currently designed in the United States, anyone who is in dire need of medical care cannot be turned away from an emergency room. Whether patients wish to pay their bill or not, they will receive treatment. This means, though we do not officially have a single-payer system in the United States, everyone pays for those who are not paying. Everyone can get care, and when some people do not pay their bills the cost of care increases for everyone else. When the Great Society reforms were designed in the 1960s, people could not afford an increased tax to the extent that would have paid for healthcare and solved this problem. The timing may have been perfect politically, but financially the country could not afford the system. According to the U.S. Census the median family's income in 1960 was only $5,600, which equates to $44,390 in 2014 dollars. The median family today earns $52,685. Over the period from 1960 to 2014, medical costs rose by more than 700%, but incomes increased by less than 25%. We may not have been able to enact such reform in 1960, but today we cannot afford not to adopt such a policy.

A New System for Healthcare

The Affordable Care Act was not the way to implement universal healthcare in the United States. The compromises that were adopted when the bill was being negotiated were obstructive and often counter to the spirit that was intended. When the bill passed it was hardly a shadow of what the president campaigned on during the election cycle. Through failed efforts to get bipartisan support, the bill was modified to the extent that it was hardly recognizable, yet bipartisan support still did not occur. Rather than keeping such a poorly designed system in place, a new system based on a similar design to the Federal Reserve System should be adopted for healthcare.

The Federal Healthcare System (FHS) should be implemented to reform healthcare and protect patients in the United States. A centralized authority, like the Federal Reserve System, removed from political whims needs to be created, commissioned, and enacted. A seven-member board of doctors could be in place with 14 year terms, appointed by the president, confirmed by the Senate, and cycled so that every two years a new board member is nominated. The board could be given purview over Medicare and Medicaid and the taxes we pay to fund those areas could be submitted directly to the new FHS for its initial operating budget.

Private doctors, hospitals, and even insurance (to fill gaps like cosmetic surgery and the like) could operate under the auspice of the new system, regulated by rules designed from the system, and accountable to the system. Tort rules could be applied from the top on an as-needed basis, designed by the experts in their field, and absent the political pressures congress currently faces. Membership fees could be required by every doctor, hospital, or insurance company and paid directly to the FHS, just like banks pay to the Federal Reserve System. An increase in the Medicare payroll tax to 5% (a rough estimate that is a little more than three times as great as the current rate and based on the population being in three categories, young, middle aged, and senior) could be implemented and matched by employers to pay additional costs that will be necessary to pay for medical care among every person in the nation.

Remove the requirement of employers to offer healthcare insurance to their employees, remit any profits the FHS earns to Social Security, and allow the healthcare system to operate as effectively as the banking and monetary system operates in the United States. Give the system four tools, co-pays to doctors, co-pays to pharmacies, tort regulation, and fee changes for member organizations. Provide the system with a tri-mandate, affordable co-pays, low healthcare inflation, and a sustainable number of medical personnel to avoid long wait times.

We can provide universal healthcare coverage in the United States, save Social Security, and improve everyone's standard of living while still keeping the median family income at $47,416 or greater after the increased payroll tax and still higher than it was in 1960 after the value conversion. Clearly what I have written about the FHS in this book is only a start to this idea; it needs major revision (for example the 5% was an off-the-cuff estimate that needs far greater analysis than I have time for in this book), but it should start a discussion. The passage of the Affordable Care Act in 2009 was equivalent to the short-term solution to the Panic of 1907 when the steel industry was allowed to monopolize; only this time it occurred for healthcare. The healthcare system in the United States needs a Jekyll Island event of its own.

It is time for a single-payer, universal healthcare system in the United States, and now our families can afford the expense. The world's largest, most advanced nation should have had it first, but since we did not, now is the time for its adoption. This nation, built on the backs of our forefathers, grandmothers, and great thinkers, tackled the turmoil of history, bled to end fascism and Stalinist-communism, and endeavored to make this nation great. There is no question of fairness. Our people worked hard to build our nation so everyone could have a greater standard of living and more easily pursue happiness. Remember, over the period from 1960 to 2014, medical costs have risen more than 28 times as fast as real income. We can't afford to ignore the growing number of problems with the healthcare system in the United States.

Minimum Wage

The wealth gap in the United States has grown to untenable levels. Wealth is defined as anything we own or assets we control and can be anything from savings accounts or real estate to stocks and bonds. The poorest 40% of all Americans control less than 0.3% of the total wealth. That means that for every $1000 in wealth in the United States, the poorest 40% control only $3. By contrast, the top 20% of Americans control 84% of the total wealth. These numbers are extremely disproportionate, and change is needed. The call for a rise in minimum wage, however, may be the wrong policy action.

Perhaps even more concerning is the income distribution in the United States. After all, income is what we use to acquire wealth. Recently Robert Reich released a movie called, *Inequality for All*. He explains how the income distribution has tilted toward the rich in growing proportions since the 1970s. It is even argued by many that we have entered a new Gilded Age, probably not as insidious as the one I discussed in the first chapter of this book, but bad nonetheless.

The answers to our previous eras of the rich getting richer and the poor getting poorer usually included protests and eventually concessions by those in power. Unions sometimes form, or existing unions speak out more aggressively. Working conditions, number of hours worked, or even the wages paid to employees are often changed to quell disagreement and return to productivity. Minimum wage was created to provide every worker a minimum, livable wage, under the auspice of the Fair Labor Standards Act of 1938. Workers could no longer be exploited by low pay and heavy work burdens. It was a groundbreaking innovation to a world in need of economic and industrial reform.

Economists have learned a lot about minimum wage and its impact on our economy since its creation. By raising minimum wage it is well known that production costs will rise. Increasing production costs drives prices higher; inflation and the cost of living rises for everyone. As the cost of living rises, the demand for higher wages increases, and eventually the legislators agree to an even higher level of minimum wage. We have been chasing a livable wage since the creation of minimum wage, and we have not yet found one. We cannot find that level because the levers we are pulling are moving all the other levers also. We pull one, another one changes. We fix the other lever and another one disrupts our original repair. Constantly seeking a higher level of minimum wage is not the answer; we can never reach a high enough level where it will stabilize and everyone will have a good, livable wage with this policy.

Leaving minimum wage at its current level is also not the answer. Poor people living on minimum wage do deserve a livable salary and a better standard of living. Since 1979 their wage has dropped, in real terms, by about $2.00 per hour[10]. They may not be college educated and they may not be writing books or blogs, but they too are productive people serving in jobs in which neither you nor I wish to work. Unfortunately, raising minimum wage is only a temporary fix to a longer term, more serious, deeply rooted problem. When minimum wage rises, prices also rise. When minimum wage is left level for a significant amount of time, the market adjusts and inflation slows but it settles above the level where minimum wage would sustain the average worker. Since 1990, no matter what the nominal wage was, it would purchase roughly the same number of goods and services, about $7.00 in real terms. That means that no matter how the wage changed, the market adjusted to match, and minimum wage workers were made no better than they were before.

More problems occur when one considers the other implications of raising minimum wage. Workers in other fields may find that flipping hamburgers or working at Wal-Mart may be more attractive than their current job. Furthermore, minimum wage employers may desire the newly available, more highly qualified workers, since they are assumed to be more productive. The worst case scenario is also the textbook case; employers will simply lay off some of their workers and not refill their positions. A surplus of available workers pressures prices downward, but the law prevents the wage from dropping and unemployment rises among those most in need. The workers we try to help by raising minimum wage will lose their jobs, and

---

[10] That's $80 per week, a car payment or half a house payment! Yet we wonder why Aggregate Demand is weak?

shortages may occur in other sectors. Raising minimum wage has far-reaching implications and is not a long-term solution. We also have to be concerned with automation too, now more than ever. Once workers become too expensive, modern technology to replace those workers may be a viable solution for employers.

Minimum wage was necessary when it was created; it is still important to ensure workers are not exploited, but overall it is obsolete in the 21st century. Unfortunately, politicians are fighting for the same old answers we've always used and are ignoring other possibilities. Temporarily we probably do need to raise minimum wage, but we should seek other options. This should be the last time we ever raise minimum wage, and it should be allowed to become an ineffective price floor and fall into obscurity.

Robert Reich recently released a shocking number relating to CEO pay. He writes, "*Until the 1980s, corporate CEOs were paid, on average, 30 times what their typical worker was paid. Since then, CEO pay has skyrocketed to 280 times the pay of a typical worker; in big companies, to 354 times*" [36]. Have the CEOs become that much more productive? No, they have not. Gabaix and Landier (2008) find very small differences between various CEOs and their talent [37]. They explain that market capitalization and the growth of business worldwide has been the justification for such large increases in CEO pay. Unfortunately, this justification is a little weak. On May 28th, 2014, the *Wall Street Journal* reported the average CEO pay was $11.4 million per year. A minimum wage worker earns just over $15,000 if they do not take a vacation (which they cannot afford anyway). That means the average CEO earns 760 times a minimum wage worker's salary. The highest paid employees in a company have been getting paid more, while the lowest paid employees are not improving.

The answer is not complicated, though it may be politically unpopular[11]. Considering that according the Bureau of Labor Statistics, only 4.3% of those paid an hourly wage in our economy are actually limited to minimum wage[12], and that among those even fewer are old enough to vote, it may be difficult to convince the lawmakers. It is important to note that many people earn more than minimum wage but are still very low in the pay scale, perhaps $9.00 per hour when minimum wage is $7.25, and these percentages do not capture that group.

The wealth and income gaps affect everyone. Even the richest members of society are negatively impacted by large wealth and income gaps. Economic mobility, crime, health, education, mental illness, and even life-span are affected by large disparities in wealth and income. From poor to rich alike, everyone suffers.

Maximum Wage Differential

The answer to fixing the wealth gap and repairing the income gap is not by redistributing wealth through taxation. Redistribution schemes are inefficient and notoriously unpopular among the population. We hope to maintain incentives and growth in businesses throughout our economy. The answer is to mandate a federal maximum wage differential. This would reduce the allowed difference between the highest paid worker and the lowest paid worker. I suggest we mandate the highest

---

[11] Unpopular ideas are not an uncommon theme in this book, it seems.
[12] This number excludes those who are retired or too young to work, and it doesn't include anyone on a salary comparable to minimum wage. This results in 4.3% being far greater than the actual number of voting, minimum wage workers.

paid employee earn no more than 50 times (Robert Reich suggested 100 times) the lowest paid domestic employee in a company, and no more than, perhaps, 200 times a foreign based employee. Each foreign nation would get a different mandated maximum and the U.S. would get a new tool for trade negotiations. I have, so far, been unable to discover any negative effects of this policy suggestion. The typical arguments usually fall to exporting jobs, increasing unemployment, and removing incentives. I will discuss these topics and the benefits such a structure would have on corporate leadership below. I will discuss the existing "old guard" CEOs and their impacts on leaving companies like Wal-Mart. Lastly I will discuss the impact on small business.

If we mandate the differential as I have stated above, then it will encourage domestic production. CEOs who wish to earn more money will be incentivized to produce inside the United States since U.S. workers earn more money, thus allowing the CEO to earn more money as well. Jobs will come home and Americans will be wealthier for the change. Domestic production will increase and unemployment will decrease. The mandate can bring jobs back to the United States. This will raise consumer prices to some extent, but higher wages will offset the harmful effects of the policy.

By minimizing the wage differential we can decrease unemployment levels through the new incentive a CEO has to expand a company. Existing CEOs may be risk averse, once they have certain stock options or yearly wages, choosing less risky ventures over growth maximizing expansions. CEOs who wish to get a raise will want to expand their businesses so they can afford to give raises to the people at the bottom of their pay structure. Providing increased pay at the bottom will allow the

CEO to get a raise at the top. Everyone in between will also benefit. Expansion means more jobs and higher pay for everyone.

The removal of incentives, as occurs with socialist movements and wealth redistribution policies, is really a moot point since this structure provides new incentives not faced before. CEOs have an incentive to expand, they have an incentive to improve productivity, and they have an incentive to pay their employees more. They have an incentive to produce domestically, and they have an incentive to make good decisions. Business owners and CEOs alike would have every incentive to make their business as profitable as they could, without the incentive to decrease pay in order to nominally increase profitability. They would have to find other, more equitable, innovative ways to save money. CEOs would need to invest in new technology, research, and education. Investment into renewable and sustainable activities would all be observable gains from such a system.

There is one somewhat valid argument I have heard against this idea , but under scrutiny it reveals a free market resolution. "Old Guard" CEOs, those who control larger or more established companies and have been around for a long time, may not wish to stay in their position since staying would mean a significant pay-cut when compared to their existing pay structure. *Let them leave.* New, innovative, more ambitious, forward-looking leadership will take over these companies. Maybe this is good for an existing company and possibly it is bad. If it's good then the companies will tip into an era of profitability they have not seen for some time. If it's bad then companies may fall into bankruptcy. If companies begin failing, for example if corporations like Wal-Mart fail, then that makes room for new corporations to compete or existing businesses to expand (just like Target supplanting K-Mart as Wal-Mart's main competitor). Either way, the system motivates fresh perspectives and new businesses to enter the marketplace.

The last argument that always enters the political-economy is how new policy affects small business. This is a tough situation, but it too has an easy answer. Any small business under a certain size, perhaps 200 employees, will not be subject to this rule. Franchises would not count, since they are under the purview of a much larger corporation, but truly small businesses should be allowed to grow until they reach a predefined tipping point. If this is unfair competition in favor of small business, so be it. According to the SBA Office of Advocacy, small business accounts for more than 64% of net new jobs created between 1993 and 2011 (11.8 million of the 18.5 million new jobs).

Other nations such as Denmark and Switzerland have already adopted similar systems to the one I propose. They have increased economic mobility, decreased wealth and income gaps, and achieved a greatly improved standard of living as a result of their changes. Their systems function well and have even spawned a joke about the American Dream. *"If Americans wish to live the American Dream, they should go to Denmark."* - Richard Wilkinson

Part 2: Temporary States, and Timing

Chapter 4: Central Planning and its Impacts

"There are those who believe that if you just legislate to make the well-to-do prosperous, that their prosperity will leak through on those below. The Democratic idea has been that if you legislate to make the masses prosperous, their prosperity will find its way up and through every class that rests upon it."
– William Jennings Bryan

Introduction to Poverty

To this point in the book I have not formally identified what it means to be in poverty, which is an important detail to discuss. One might view poverty as an easily escapable reality through the simple application of hard work and a good work ethic. One may believe that impoverished people could simply go get a job, stop buying cigarettes, drugs or alcohol, or work harder – as so many others have – to achieve a better material existence and improved standard of living. Saving more and wasting less may be the golden key to obtaining prosperity. Even the famous billionaire, Kevin O'Leary recently stated, *"If you work hard, you might be stinking rich one day"* when discussing the more than 1 billion people living on less than $1.50 per day. This idea is so permeating that many Americans may even be unsettled by the United States government sending billions of dollars in aid to foreign nations and peoples each year.

It is true that the United States government spends nearly $50 billion each year on foreign aid, but redirecting that aid to U.S. infrastructure projects or tax breaks would not even begin to measurably affect an American's life, not even for the poorest among us. Fifty billion dollars equates to only about $160 per person, per year in the United States. The Department of Health and Human Services in the United States considers one who earns less than $11,490 per year, or just over $31 per day, impoverished [38]. So spending $160 per person would pay for less than six days of existence for those living in what we define as poverty in the United States. Comparably, it would pay for 50 days of existence for all who earn less than $1.00 per day in our world.

Foreign aid is also important to national security, diplomatic relations, and to helping those in far worse need than Americans. Perhaps domestic investment, redirecting the aid to something like infrastructure spending, might be a good idea. However, the good will the aid generates, the better political environment it creates – the improved standards of living and impact to people's lives it inspires – also has a national security aspect. Jeffrey Sachs summed it up, *"Whether terrorists are rich or poor or middle class, their staging areas – their bases of operation – are unstable societies beset by poverty, unemployment, rapid population growth, hunger, and lack of hope"* [2]. Our foreign aid can mitigate these symptoms, and keep this country safe while also alleviating the suffering of billions of people.

Investing in America is always a good idea, but investing elsewhere can be beneficial for Americans too. Remember, even the poorest American who lives on approximately $31 per day may be lucky enough to have other, in-kind (payments other than cash) services such as cable television, Internet, food, clean water, air-conditioning and heating, a soft bed, a relatively clean environment, protection of law, private property rights, free education, access to higher education, and much more.

The impoverished people of the world, often defined as the bottom billion (the most impoverished nations of the world where approximately one billion people currently reside were identified by Paul Collier as the "Bottom Billion" countries), live on less than $1.50 per day. They likely do not have clean water; they often lack food, and they do not have luxuries like television, Internet, air-conditioning, or heating. Many cook on wood stoves that do not have proper ventilation; the smoke causes respiratory problems and further intensifies their impoverished existence through disease. These people lack protection from criminal elements and sometimes even their own governments. If you, the reader, are doing the math, *the poorest people in the United States are living on nearly 20 times the real income of the bottom billion people in the world.* Sadly, even that number does not include the value of the in-kind products, infrastructure, protections, and health effects listed above, which would surely increase Americans' wealth dramatically.

We take the protection from invasion from both foreign and domestic invaders for granted. Many impoverished nations' populations have to be concerned over how their neighbors treat them and how their own government mistreats them. They live with an uncertainty about whether their home may be burgled or possibly even confiscated by their own government. Primary education is sometimes inaccessible (if/when it is available at all) and children are often sent to work instead of school. In the developed world we have legal recourse for abuse from an employer who simply uses inappropriate words. By contrast in the most impoverished nations, the bottom billion nations, workers may not even have recourse if their managers decide to beat or sexually abuse them.

Much of the world still utilizes child labor, abuses lower classes, and degrades the rights of women. Given the chance to work to improve their lives, these women are eager for the opportunity. In *The End of Poverty*, Jeffrey Sachs discusses women working in the garment industry of Bangladesh. He writes, *"...they recounted the arduous hours, lack of labor rights, and the harassment. What was most striking and unexpected about the stories was the repeated affirmation that this work was the greatest opportunity that these women could ever have imagined, and that their employment had changed their lives for the better"* [2]. These women had not been poor in their previous circumstances because of an unwillingness to work or learn. They were not failing to save or invest time, money or effort. The children of these women were not starving because their mothers had simply chosen poverty over wealth. They did not lack creativity and they were not lazy. These women were poor because they had previously lacked opportunity and they did not live in the right geographic location where jobs were abundant, or the right type of political environment where they could create their own opportunities. This is the state of a large portion of our world.

Poverty is not new, though its face has changed over time. Poverty is not natural, though it has existed in all parts of human history. There is a long list of people who have attempted to alleviate the plight that is poverty. The problem has been acknowledged and addressed by all three of the economists this book has discussed: Friedrich Hayek, John Maynard Keynes, and Karl Marx. The elimination of poverty and the improvement of all humankind is a big part of the reason we study Economics, *The Dismal Science*. Our goal is to find the proper incentives that motivate markets and enable people to harness improved standards of living and national growth world-wide, bettering the lives of others and our own lives by extension. Everyone should hope to end world poverty, if not for those suffering the most then at least for themselves; worldwide economic improvement is a circular and symbiotic relationship. Ending world poverty helps everyone.

Adopting proper policies and more effective forms of government at all levels is necessary to affect change on the poorest peoples in this world. Poverty can be eradicated but we must find a correct, sustainable solution that has eluded so many of our leaders, economists, and philanthropists for far too many centuries. We must also remember that the state of the economy where we attempt to employ a solution must be deeply evaluated, since not every solution is viable under every set of economic circumstances. Our solutions must be focused and relevant, efficient and effective, and customized to the state of affairs in each of the nations and communities where we intervene. We must not ignore any idea or ideology, no matter how unpopular the idea, entrenched the ideology, or powerful the opposition. The problem is not simple and there is no singular, master solution – there are many.

The Ebb and Flow

Karl Marx proposed government ownership over the means of production, with the hope of achieving a more equitable distribution of wealth among the population of a nation. He advocated that every industrialized nation would move toward socialist policies in time – if not absolute socialism – and that capitalism was only a temporary state for the world's nations on their way toward a utopian society. His arguments were compelling enough to lead many of the greatest economists of the early 20th century to advocate for government ownership over all the means of production and direct controls over prices and wages, and many nations followed the recommended protocols. With the help of charismatic leaders like Vladimir Lenin and ripe economic conditions following World War I, workers around the world demanded a change from the capitalism that was, seemingly, failing to put food on their tables.

Free markets had offered much by creating jobs, inventions, and innovations for the use of new technologies. All society had been improving for more than a century, from Europe to Asia and the Americas. Farm yields had improved, industrial production had increased, and world trade had been thriving. Capitalist markets, however, had created unpredictable business cycles leading to more inequality and increasing wealth-gaps. The greed of the industrialists had led to nations growing more powerful, the emergence of "Robber Barons," and though it had parented invention and innovation, it also had a dark side. Even today the dark side of industrialism is rearing its ugly head in developing nations such as China, where worker abuse is common and human rights are often ignored [39] [40].

The greed of the industrialists that had created so many new jobs and employed so many people who were unemployed before, had also led to large wealth gaps and sometimes dangerous working conditions. The free market had failed to address the greed and abuse created by unfettered marketeers. It increasingly seemed natural that the government would step in to regulate markets or flatly seize businesses where workers had been abused, degraded, or exploited. Many thought that through government ownership over the means of production, the leadership could control prices and wages and ensure every person in a nation could be made equal, able to acquire appropriate levels of housing and nutrition. Many began to believe that poverty could be eliminated through the changes Karl Marx had proposed. *"Workers of the world unite,"* was the battle-cry for those hoping to achieve these dreams. As workers unionized and protested, governments began to react through political change; sometimes even violent uprisings led to immediate change. Socialism – and even communism – was acquiring a foothold in many of the world's economies.

Violent uprisings which led to communism [41] are not, however, a long-term, sustainable solution to the affliction of the under-privileged, and a gradual transition will not work under all conditions either. Given the conditions of the world when Marx wrote his famous works, *The Communist Manifesto* and *Das Kapital*, it likely seemed natural to think that economies would eventually change from capitalism into socialism. After all, history had already shown an evolution from old ideas to new ones; anarchy gave way to feudalism which eventually capitulated to Enlightenment thinking, Republican forms of government, and capitalist markets. Under the conditions which Marx wrote, it probably seemed like capitalism may shift toward socialism. The world had changed dramatically over the course of centuries; socialism did not exist at the time, and the natural evolution of an economy seemed to have no other option – short of remaining capitalist – than to evolve past capitalism and into some other, new form of political economy. Since socialism was the latest idea, the conclusion Marx reached still appears logical. However, he never considered that once socialism was adopted it might eventually lead back to a capitalist outcome, or that its adoption might increase the incidence of poverty where it ruled. Socialism, according to Marx, was the final step on the path toward utopianism.

Marx had ignored the one necessary input for economic growth and an improved standard of living for everyone – incentives. It probably felt rather natural to think people would eventually overcome their greed and wish to work for the betterment of humanity, thus moving from capitalism toward socialism. Even the more modern thinker Gene Roddenberry created *Star Trek* with a very similar idea. Without incentives, however, people lacked motivation and a state of low productivity took hold in the communist nations of the world.

Research examining purely socialist governments reveals great inefficiencies produced by such a system [42] [43] David Miller put it succinctly, *"The evidence, badly summarized, is that no socialist state has yet succeeded in gearing production to the needs of its population without, on the one hand, creating surpluses of unwanted goods and, on the other, forcing people to rely on black marketeering, bureaucratic string-pulling, and so forth to get the goods they do want; nor has the quality of goods produced matched that achieved in the capitalist market economies."* The sentiment is as true today as it was when he wrote it in 1977. The betterment of humanity is not always the best incentive to induce invention, investment, innovation, and entrepreneurship.

In reality it seems Marx's ideas have historically been utilized under improper conditions. When the market is functioning properly there is no reason to intervene in the system; government can be laissez-faire, markets will grow, and citizens are made better off through natural mechanisms. Economic activity will organize and redistribute goods and services from lower-valued uses to higher-valued uses, and no centrally planned redistribution model is necessary. Once markets grow for a while and weaknesses become evident, government intervention may be necessary to avoid market failures, assure a more equitable distribution of wealth, and for the improvement on everyone's standard of living. Driving all the way to absolute socialism, however, is only rarely prescribed and certainly not for the long term treatment of a poorly functioning economy.

Increasing poverty or economic malfunction has two basic prescriptions:

1. Adopt socialist policies temporarily and drive toward free markets, ending with a mixed economy.
2. Adopt free market policies permanently and drive toward socialism, ending with a mixed economy.

There are many caveats to the two prescriptions above, and once a mixed economy is adopted there may be minor changes to be made. Only the conditions of the economy can dictate what policy changes are necessary. It is entirely possible the leadership might correctly find that driving more toward free markets or even socialism is the right objective under particular circumstances. Policy makers must make those decisions only after they acquire the data to inform their decisions.

Adopt Socialism Convert to Capitalism

As I go through this exercise with you, the reader, it is important to keep in mind that the following is the evolution of an idea in an ideal world. In reality the implementation of any major political or economic change is far more complicated and cumbersome than can be written in a few pages of a book – perhaps not even in a whole book. I will describe my solution for manageably undertaking this idea later in this chapter, but for now it is only meant to explain how socialism *could* lead to capitalism and well-functioning, active markets.

Adopting socialism could be a temporary means to an end in nations where markets have failed to emerge and reallocate resources efficiently, or where any of the factors of production is missing. Marx assumed nations would move from capitalism and into socialism, but nations may also opt to become socialist before adopting policies that make it a productive, market-driven economy – even while maintaining some socialist command over various sectors like health, banking, or infrastructure. Though socialism is inherently inefficient, a socialist government may obtain and control all the factors of production until those inefficiencies become evident – ultimately replacing missing factors with government support. Through central planning, the factors of production can be redirected, productive resources can be built and fully utilized, and a previously non-productive society can be made productive. Natural resources can be properly developed but not pillaged, factories can be built not abandoned, local businesses can be created not discouraged, the population can become employed not indentured, and the entire economy can become productive not plundered.

Inefficiencies will become evident relatively quickly, since governments are always unable to maintain a perfect redistribution of resources. Overinvestment in some sectors will lead to underinvestment in others. The leadership will do its best to maintain some sort of control, but eventually it will be clear the government cannot effectively manage the entire economy. In the words of William Easterly, *"You Cannot Plan a Market."* Small businesses, for example, are created at the community level and the government will likely have trouble managing the commanding heights while also directing the activities on the wide array of markets that exist on the granulated, micro scale.

Before giving up control over businesses, however, the government must have a legal system in place, with understandable, enforceable, and culturally-sensitive laws for civil and criminal cases. Courts are necessary for the enforcement of contracts and to guarantee legal ownership. Small businesses cannot operate effectively in any environment without the protection of law; they definitely will not grow, and entrepreneurs will not invest. Small businesses will not have the ability to acquire financial capital from investors or banks as long as their rights to property are not well-defined and protected. Courts will have to be created and land-titling will have to be adopted before the government can shift to a free market driven economy.

The next step is for the government to give up control over small businesses and allow natural, market production and pricing mechanisms to emerge. The pricing mechanism of a free market is far superior to a central planner for relaying information to consumers. Relative scarcity of goods and services will reallocate entrepreneurs and consumers to invest and purchase items in the most needed sectors. Through the market mechanism, labor and consumption goods and services are redirected to the consumers and suppliers who value them most – low valued uses to higher valued uses. The famous father of modern economics, Adam Smith, called this automatic reallocation of goods and services, *"the invisible hand."* Agents acting in the economy in their own self-interests will inevitably benefit society-at-large through their market activities. Socially desirable businesses will remain in operation while socially undesirable businesses will go bankrupt. As the invisible hand is allowed to function, national policy moves from pure socialism toward mixed capitalism.

Once property rights are clearly and simply defined and courts are created for enforcement of those rights and contractual agreements, the leadership will have no reason not to allow the formation and self-direction of small businesses within communities, as well as market-driven prices from those businesses. Allowing markets to operate freely will be less demanding on the leadership, less expensive for the government, and more efficient than central planning. Additionally, given that general stores and grocers are vital to the health of any community, ensuring local entrepreneurs' freedom to succeed is important to the continuing development of the impoverished world. Freer markets will ensure economic resources will be utilized more fully.

After the micro scale markets are freed, the industrial sector will have to be addressed. Entrepreneurs sell to consumer markets and buy from factor markets; thus, a reactive industrial sector is key to their success. Small businesses will demand various inputs be produced for their conversion into consumer goods. If the government does not act swiftly enough, small businesses will suffer and possibly fail, making all the previous efforts for naught. Since governments are notoriously bureaucratic, non-reactionary and slow, the government will have to begin the process of privatizing industry and agriculture after small businesses begin to form and are properly protected by law. If government maintains tight controls over industry, does not guarantee private property rights, and does not fulfill market demands for production, then sectors of the economy will begin to fail, economic growth will slow, and development will be hindered. Without proper businesses there are no legally operating markets and legal economic activity will cease, which will cause a slide back into under-development.

A reliable flow of inputs from industry will also improve small businesses' credibility with banks. In the developing world banking is incredibly important; there is a shortage of banks available to poorer communities and access to capital development is difficult to find. Now that the government has begun the privatization process, it can begin creating a centralized bank. This central bank can be responsible for the development of local banks around the country, and the formation of capital. The central bank should be regulated by the government, but privately controlled to avoid over-monetizing the nation and creating hyperinflationary pressures. Once private property rights are pervasive, small businesses are operating, pricing is decentralized, industrial production is moving forward and held privately, and a banking system is entrusted with monetary policy, the population can begin borrowing to invest in capital equipment, buildings, and technology. Tax revenues will increase and the government can finally invest into improved infrastructure.

The final step is to encourage foreign direct investment. By creating many of the systems above, guaranteeing private property, properly titling land, and ensuring the safety of assets, a friendly business environment is finally present. Once that environment is created then the nation can begin acting to bring in foreign-owned industry. Developing nations can utilize many encouraging policies such as lower taxes on production, decreased export costs, or fewer trade barriers to encourage FDI (Foreign Direct Investment). Nations can even advertise their abundance of cheap labor in comparison to the industrialized world. When foreign investors find a friendly place to build their factories with an abundant, cheap labor supply and reliable inputs, they will be happy to build their production facilities there. The seeds of growth have been sewn – and it all began within a socialist regime.

This evolution from pure socialism into pure capitalism is not the entire story, it is only the beginning. Remember, Karl Marx was observing the move toward utopianism from the perspective of an industrialized nation, not a developing one. This process is relatively accurate from the perspective of a developing nation, but once a nation has industrialized the evolution is somewhat different. At that point it is time to move toward at least a few socialist policies. The most intriguing thing for me is that an industrialized nation should never become entirely socialist, but it makes sense to become entirely socialist for a developing nation. As long as a nation progresses *from* socialism *to* capitalism, it will grow wealthier. Once a nation acquires a certain level of wealth, it makes sense a wealthy nation will adopt socialist policies to protect public health and improve infrastructure.

Individual forms of socialism may never be eliminated, but, again, a mixed form of market socialism may emerge. Depending on the state of the world at any particular point in history, the culture where the state is ruling, and the conditions of the economy, it may become necessary for a nation to move away from market-socialism and into pure socialism or pure capitalism for a short time. What matters most is the state of the world at the time policies are chosen and the state of the economy where those policies are adopted. There are many political and economic factors that I have left out above, but the point is clear – the state of the world, the position of the nation's economy, and the will of the people all matter when a final decision is made. No one ideology is correct under all economic conditions.

It is more realistic to consider that every idea of economics can be correct under the right economic conditions and that they will also lead to every other extreme under other circumstances. Socialism is not any more extreme than any other form of political economy. The three main ideas, socialism, free market capitalism, and market socialism, exist on a continuum that can be visualized in the form of a triangle. Socialism can lead to capitalism, and sometimes this may be necessary. Capitalism can lead to socialism, and sometimes this may be necessary in the short term. They are both more likely to reach some sort of mixed arrangement that is far more stable in the long term – market socialism. However, as economic conditions change, different policies become more relevant and existing policies may fall into obscurity.

Adopt Capitalism and Convert toward Socialism

Winston Churchill once said, *"The inherent vice of capitalism is the unequal sharing of blessings; the inherent virtue of socialism is the equal sharing of miseries."* Incentives are certainly the best way to redirect the efforts of human activity, and prices are definitely the most efficient way of rationing earth's scarce resources. The unfortunate truth is that the incentives faced by private business are sometimes in direct opposition to the public good and other scarce resources may be harmed during production. It is difficult or impossible to include the negative externalities industry sometimes creates within the price of consumer goods being produced and sold. Businesses create jobs, new technology, and make our lives better, to be sure. However, corporations' primary objective is to make a profit for their shareholders. Sometimes profit comes at the expense of some other system, ecological or otherwise.

If the wealth gap between the richest 20% of people and the poorest 20% of people grows too large[13], or if the free market and private industry fails to address particular public issues, the job of government is made clear. Issues may include things like environmental protection, education, or public health, and society at large may demand a change that the market is ignoring. The proper policy to address the exact issues may not be as transparent, unfortunately, but it is still the job of the legislature to have the discussion and search for the appropriate response to market failures. In extreme circumstances, populations may even decide it is necessary for the government to take over particular portions of the economy that are under-provided by private industry or the free market.

Programs for environmental protection, monetary policy and centralized banking, universal education and healthcare, enforcement of private property rights and contracts enforcement, basic infrastructure, local policing, and national defense are better for government to provide than private industries of the free market. When left to private markets, industry has every incentive to maximize profits and minimize costs; for example, when it is costly for the industry to reduce environmental impact it faces an incentive to pollute. We even find it written in textbooks that outsourcing sometimes occurs because of easier environmental regulations in developing nations. Since markets are so diffuse, the typical consumer in one part of a nation may be uninformed about the environmental abuses of a corporation in another part of the same nation, thereby mitigating the miniscule amount of market power the consumer does have. Globalization exacerbates this same issue. Thus, people continue to purchase environmentally abusive

---

[13] when discussing wealth gaps it is common among textbooks and economists to compare the top 20% of earners to the bottom 20%

firms' products and the abusive firms continue their harmful activities. Therefore, a move toward socialist policies becomes necessarily ascendant.

As time has progressed, world trade has grown more ubiquitous. A very large portion of our consumer goods are made or assembled in other nations like China, for example. Yet citizens in western countries, who are not exposed to poor practices that perpetuate things like human rights abuses, smog, or water pollution and are often associated with unregulated markets, continue to purchase goods labeled "Made in [Country]." It is difficult for western consumers to gauge the effects of abuses in such a distant place; therefore, consumers largely ignore the distant labor and environmental exploitation that often leads to disasters and human rights abuses.

It is in the interest of society as a whole to retain a clean and healthy environment. Yet environmental protection will be under-provided in an economy where such protection is left entirely to free markets and industry by extension. A healthy planet, with clean air and clean water, leads to improved public health, greater economic growth, and generally improved productivity for everyone [44]. Clean production is unfortunately often costly to firms; therefore, it is frequently under-prioritized. Since industries will experience few consequences from their activities if they ignore environmental impacts, and because their competitors may also ignore said impacts, industrial producers are left with little choice except to pollute or exploit labor if they desire to remain competitive. Since exploitation of environment and labor is not readily apparent to the distant consumers, and because market power is too granulated for the population to have a true, market-based recourse, the government is the only place left to turn.

As a result of world economic growth, four of the twelve most polluted rivers in the world exist in India and China. Consumers may not be directly affected by these environmental abuses today, but eventually they will. Whether it is the rising acidity of the ocean that depletes fisheries, chemical spills that destroy local habitats and shrimping, fertilizer runoff that creates dead-zones (regions of water without oxygen), or a rising sea-level due to global climate-change, environmental abuses will eventually be evident for everyone. By then, however, it will be too late to make the necessary changes. Only governments can take action to mandate a stop to the abuses, since it is corporate suicide to unilaterally adopt cleaner production practices.

Taxpayer funded public education leads to decreasing income inequality and declining levels of poverty [45]. Educating every child in a society can also be directly correlated to increased wages [46] [47] and, by extension, greater economic output and increased aggregate demand. If society should choose not to educate young people, or be unable to educate them, the workforce would retain a lower level of human capital resulting in a less productive, less innovative, less inventive, and generally less prosperous society. Adam Smith even addressed this concern, *"The expense of the institutions for education and religious instruction, is likewise, no doubt, beneficial to the whole society, and may, therefore, without injustice, be defrayed by the general contribution of society."* In other words, education should be publicly provided.

Without public education, corporations would be forced to search for employees from a pool of less-skilled workers; thus, their output would suffer, wages would remain low, and poverty would be intensified. Businesses could opt to train their new employees, but 12 years of education can be costly both for the business and the employee, not only in explicit dollar costs, but also in terms of lost wages and production. Left to private investment, education would be under-provided, at least until corporations learned – assuming they would learn – that educating everyone may lead to greater productivity and improved profit margins in the long-term.

Sometimes proximity to capital is all that is necessary for great visionaries to fulfill their full potential. Bill Gates was publicly educated but he grew up in Seattle where he had access to computers. As a kid, he would often sneak out of his parents' house at night to write computer programs at the University of Washington [48]. Bill Gates did not need a college degree to create Microsoft; in fact, he did not even finish college, though he did earn an honorary doctorate from Harvard in 2007. What Bill Gates did need, however, was proximity to a computing center and access to the proper capital to learn how to program. Without a government that had invested in human capital for all young people, and without proper systems that promoted growth and investment, the computers Gates learned on may never have been built or located near his home. Certainly the probability of Bill Gates getting a primary or secondary education would have declined if it had not been subsidized by the government. If Gates had grown up in Ethiopia, for example, where education does not permeate every community, he may never have learned to write computer programs, and Windows may not exist as we know it today. Imagine the lost productivity, in terms of both time and money, if Microsoft did not exist!

Improved public health is also important to growth and the reduction of poverty. The less healthy a society, the less productive the people become, and increasing rates of poverty is the result. When otherwise able-bodied adults are rendered ill or disabled, normal activities such as farming or industrial production decline. Nations that do not invest in the well-being of their citizens will inevitably exist with increased rates of starvation and disease and will likely incur subsistence levels of existence. In those nations there may not be enough technology or human capital available to enable the free markets to reduce the incidence of disease or to improve public health. There may not be enough educated doctors or trained nurses to treat the ill and the opportunity for wealth may be too small to encourage the large investment it takes to become a doctor. Western doctors who seek wealth will stay in the West, and the charitable organizations may be unable to provide enough doctors or nurses to treat at the levels necessary to assist in the creation of prosperity. In Ethiopia, just too quickly display this point, the World Bank does not even register enough doctors to report a good measurement and lists 0.0 doctors per 1000 population. The free market under-provides the medical personnel, growth slows as the population is sicker and weaker overall [49], and poverty is perpetuated.

Basic infrastructure is another place where governments should invest instead of private free markets. The classic example is that of the lighthouse, first introduced by John Stuart Mill. Mill claimed that lighthouses would be under-provided since there would be no way to extract payment from random ships arriving from foreign ports, and if they were privately held then trade would be inhibited by tolls on waterways. Therefore, there would be no incentive for privately-owned lighthouses to be built, and their private construction may be harmful to trade routes. This argument was debunked later, however, when it was revealed that the majority of the lighthouses in England were, in reality, privately owned [50].Business owners in local ports formed organizations to enforce agreements for the cost of lighthouses, since they found them beneficial. Owners of local businesses would place an additional fee on top of the price of their goods, and the local lighthouse owner would receive funding from sales to ships who docked in the port [50].

The under-provision of lighthouses, however, is a bit of a misnomer. John Stuart Mill's argument is still valid for some public goods. Building and operating a lighthouse may be expensive and time-consuming, but it is nowhere near the level of treasure and manpower necessary for the building of highways, modern ports, sanitation systems, and water transmission pipes. Since roads are important for the sale of homes in housing developments, it is true that contractors will often build roads in urban areas they are developing and then sell or donate the roads to local governments. If it was profitable for the builders to maintain control over the roads, we can be sure they certainly would. The maintenance over such structures is simply too expensive to justify the investment. If the neighborhoods wished to organize and pay a homeowner's fee to maintain their roads, the roads would be maintained. These organizations sound quite similar to governments and the fees sound quite similar to taxes, however. Allowing such organizations to exist on a street by street, neighborhood by neighborhood basis would increase administrative costs and be incredibly inefficient. In this example the free market is the inefficient system; managing such a system on a neighborhood by neighborhood basis would be far more expensive than a single government entity. Just like letting the lighthouse owner charge every individual ship that came into port would be terribly inefficient, a local government or organization can significantly reduce such a transaction cost. Letting the local government take over this responsibility is better for everyone involved.

If the government would not pay for maintenance, or could not afford to pay for maintenance, private industries would have little incentive to build the structures, and they might be under-provided in the economy. It would not, for example, be effective to allow corporations to build highways, and only a few industries have enough profitability to justify such a major investment. The use of the highways would almost certainly be restricted or tolled, and the ownership would be monopolistic in nature – perhaps even justified by the natural monopoly phenomenon. With such a large investment to recoup and the cost of maintenance always present, the price for utilizing the structure would be high, and it is possible the general population would be impeded, if not completely restricted, from accessing such infrastructure. Interstate and intrastate trade would decline as the cost of transport would rise; growth would slow, travel would be inhibited, and our standard of living would fall. Government provision for unfettered access to highways is important for government, corporations, and civilians alike. President Dwight D. Eisenhower said, *"More than any single action by the government since the end of the war, this one would change the face of America with straightaways, cloverleaf turns, bridges, and elongated parkways. Its impact on the American economy—the jobs it would produce in manufacturing and construction, the rural areas it would open up—was beyond calculation."*

Access to clean water and sanitation is also important and is under-provided by markets. According to the World Bank, in 2008, 40% of the world does not have proper improved sanitation facilities [51]. In fact, 1.5 million children are reported to die every year as a direct result of poor sanitation and contaminated water sources [51]. While the free market may, in time, provide such systems, they have not yet proven to do so in the developing world. Clean water is directly related to health, and poor sanitation is directly correlated with disease. Banerjee and Duflo write, *"The introduction of piped water, better sanitation, and chlorination of water sources was responsible for something like three-fourths of the decline in infant mortality between 1900 and 1946 and nearly half the overall reduction in mortality over the same period"* [52]. Sickness and death are directly correlated with weak growth and decreased living standards, which lead to decreased wealth and decreased incentive for investment.

With such a large portion of the world lacking such basic services as clean water and sanitation, it would seem the free market has not provided the necessary systems and that government intervention is necessary. Where people are poor, investors do not commit their riches; infrastructure does not develop through market activities since few market activities exist, and private property rights are not pervasive. Entire regions of the world remain in a terrible state of poverty while they wait for markets to emerge.

In wealthier nations private markets may play an important role in the creation of private security forces and possibly even national defense. The problem exists where people are unable to pay for their own security and where private property is not protected from intruders or bandits. Public expenditures on police to enforce private ownership will provide an innate security that allows working-aged adults to leave their belongings and undertake productive activities. Public spending on courts will ensure rights to property are protected and contracts are enforced. Protecting private property rights through police and courts will provide an incentive for populations to invent, innovate, invest, and improve (the four i's) their region of the world. When there is no public expenditure on police and courts, poorer people are forced to spend resources (time and money) to protect their property, and they do not have the proper level of development or motivation for the four i's to flourish. Most impoverished people do not have the wealth to spend on any meaningful private security, which results in less time spent on their occupations, slowing production and economic growth, and pushes their incomes even lower.

Lower income populations are unable to buy many goods and services. With lower demand, industries are forced to reduce production – or never to invest in production at all – and supply shifts downward. Unemployment increases as businesses invest elsewhere, further decreasing demand and intensifying the poverty of the population. The problems become greater as the spiral continues downward. It is possible private companies would see this problem and unilaterally choose to invest in a local police force since it is in their interest to maximize profits by improving local labor inputs. The lack of evidence that such investment occurs frequently in the developing world, however, makes this claim dubious. Investment into local policing is under-provided, and local economies continue to suffer.

The military is another example of a public good that would be under-provided if left to private markets to purchase. Any single company that might choose to spend money on military expenditures would also be defending other local industries and possibly even competitors. Spending money to defend a competitor would drive expenses higher and create an advantage for the competitor who does not have the same expense. Since other industries would assume there will be a military whether they pay for a portion of the cost or not, they are likely to free-ride on the existing military provided by other industries, particularly their competitors. Since every corporation in every industry is likely to reach the same conclusion – namely that everyone has a strategic interest in free-riding – it is likely the military will experience underinvestment – if it exists at all. The risk of coup is already high in the developing world and private militaries do sometimes emerge. These events only deepen the existing problem associated with private investment into military organizations. Surely it can be agreed that the military should only be created, operated, and maintained by a functioning government.

The capitalist economy will never be eliminated in this particular evolutionary path, but a mixed form of market-socialism may emerge. Through the provision of necessary public goods, people would find the job of government clearly defined. Where the market fails to invest, the government should intervene to produce what is under-provided through market actions. Government-provided goods are desirable socially, but it is not desirable to be the only entity providing those goods and every free market participant has an incentive to free-ride. The government is the only entity which desires to pay for goods that are under-provided in the market at large. Additionally – and most importantly – where private property rights are not clearly defined, the government needs to define them and subsequently protect them with police and courts.

There is no need for the government to take over every aspect of every citizen's life, nor to own every part of the means of production. Furthermore, central planning is *always* inefficient in the long-run. Markets need to freely operate until market weaknesses are elucidated, and in that new illumination the government will find purpose. The government should not control the "Commanding Heights" of the economy indefinitely, and in industrialized economies the government should never control the means of production. However, government should certainly own, maintain, and control at least the socially desirable systems listed above and in previous chapters when they are under-provided by market participants.

Decentralization and Free Trade

Governments of the world have learned how to gain from freer trade. Whether they adopt mercantilist policy, manipulative monetary policy, or simply remove tariffs and quotas and open their nations to international markets, almost every nation seems to have joined in the global marketplace. People all over the world are beginning to realize that by improving the standards of living for others, their standard of living increases as well. Whether they get cheaper consumer products, better technologies, cultural exposure, or if jobs come when their village gains a new factory, everyone benefits when poor people are made into consumers and rich people are able to safely invest. To that end, many nations are lowering trade barriers and encouraging foreign investment. Free trade zones are emerging all over the world and specialization, the idea Adam Smith first championed way back in 1776, is promoting a more abundant, progressive, and prosperous world.

The Bolshevik revolution, led by Vladimir Lenin in 1917, was the first step toward converting Tsarist Russia into the Soviet state we were familiar with throughout much of the 20th century. Ultimately the Bolsheviks became the communist party of the Soviet Union, leading to the international mistrust that finally pushed them into the Cold War. The Cold War, which unofficially began in 1947, saw the Soviet Union shunned from trade with Europe, the United States, and other minor U.S. and

European allies. As their share of world trade shrank and the Soviet economy and the economy of her allies suffered, the USSR eventually became impoverished.

Small business was virtually eliminated and often made illegal under the Soviet regime. Public resources were also inefficiently redirected throughout various parts of the economy. The centrally-planned model often ignored the needs of the people, such as common comforts, and focused on the prestige of the nation. Looking at the local level of the Soviet Union, one may not have been surprised to see abject poverty. Looking from the outside however, one may marvel at the Soviet Union's advanced space program, industrial development, and mighty military. This observation only gives credence to the argument that the market cannot be planned. The leadership was very successful in creating heavy industry, scientific discovery, and military superiority. The communists were unable to capitalize on those gains however, since they were excluded from large portions of world trade.

The inefficiency of Soviet command-style economic planning becomes further evident when we examine how the Soviet government consolidated many of its programs, such as agriculture, industry, and technology. Groups of smaller farms were united into mega farms, for example, because larger farms were easier to manage and capital equipment could be better utilized to make farming more efficient. In the process of consolidation, private property over land was almost entirely eliminated. At one point during the Soviet Union, 3% of the farms, the ones allowed to be privately held, provided over 50% of the agricultural products for the nation [41]. This type of centrally-planned model is not what Marx had originally intended; Stalin had taken his ideas to the extreme.

Unfortunately many other nations also followed the Soviet model.

In 1949, Mao Zedong led a communist revolution in China. Chinese producers had been hoarding grain while speculating that grain prices would rise and windfall profits might be realized. Facing famine, Chairman Mao eventually won the civil war and attained power over the starving nation. Upon marching into various villages he was astounded to find hundreds of tons of rotting grain that was now unusable. The market mechanism that had incentivized certain wealthy families to hoard their grain led to revolt and the end of the Chinese market based system [53].

The Chinese economy adopted communist and isolationist policies under Mao, who undertook the Great Leap Forward in 1958, when he planned to modernize China. During the Great Leap Forward, Chinese farmers were repurposed to produce steel in back-yard steel smelters. Famine reared its head again and the effort for China to industrialize is credited with the death of more than 40 million Chinese citizens by some accounts [54]. By the time of his death in 1976, the Chinese economy was still suffering but a large infrastructure and industrial base had been built, to Mao's credit – though the cost in human lives versus the benefit to future generations should be questioned. A few years later, after a short power struggle between restorationists and reformers (essentially Stalinists and Capitalists, respectively), they began progressing toward more trade-friendly policies. Though the Mao era was a human rights disaster, with the infrastructure and industrial base Mao commissioned, China is now able to participate in trade on a global scale. China is now (2014) the United States' second (to Canada) largest trading partner.

As nations continue to open up their borders and adopt free trade policies, the peoples of the world benefit as standards of living continue to rise. As the U.S. imports from China, Chinese workers acquire employment and American consumers can afford less expensive goods. As U.S. producers export to Canada and Mexico, American producers employ American workers, and the Canadian and Mexican peoples are able to afford less expensive goods than they themselves were able to produce. Nations specialize in their respective comparative advantages, and gains from trade are improving peoples' lives all over the world.

Circumstances that led countries to adopt what were in hindsight bad policies were necessary at various points in history. Given the situation in each nation even authoritarianism might have sometimes been justified. When the Roman Republic converted to an Empire, there had been a power vacuum and corruption was abundant. The Empire eventually fell after centuries of human rights abuses and poor governance. Feudalism emerged during the dark ages and was the best system available to organize food production and security until it became obsolete during the Enlightenment. Change is always difficult, especially systemic change, but as time progresses difficult choices, compromises, and new diagnoses will always lead to better outcomes in the future. Sometimes poor governance and experimentation illuminate better or worse systems, but each of those systems may have been necessary at the time they were adopted.

Chapter 5: Temporary or Permanent

*"... there is always a well-known solution to every human
problem – neat, plausible, and wrong."*
– Henry Louis Mencken

Sudden or Gradual – Which is Best?

The Soviet Union was dissolved in 1991 and a capitalist society emerged in its place. Other nations began to sign trade agreements with Russia, and the nation found access to world markets very beneficial. Most recently, for example, Russia signed a trade deal with China that was one of the largest such deals in the history of the world. At $400 billion, the deal promises to improve the economies of both Russia and China for the next 30 years. Other former Soviet states have also begun shifting from exclusively regional trade and are now participating in trade ranging from farm products to energy all across the globe.

There is no shortage of evidence to support the argument that communism and socialist policies are bad for a country. There is not a single example of a communist state, other than China, that has developed and thrived while it remained communist (though one may argue that non-seclusionist policies and access to world markets played an important role for China's success). China is the only example of a socialist state that has grown economically and acquired a large share of global trade while still under communist leadership. There are no industrialized nations that have ever successfully achieved long-term growth while under socialist rule or via centralized planning and increased government interventions in their economy. However, this is only half the story. Some nations have emerged from socialist planning with a developing infrastructure, political power structure, and the necessary seeds for economic growth, assuming that change was gradual. Shock Therapy[14], for example, resulted in another 10 to 15 year period of slow growth for most nations who adopted such policies.

Morgan Stanley has identified 21 emerging market economies in the world (MSCI index - 2014). Of the 21 emerging economies of the world, only eight have previously existed with large amounts of central planning, socialism, or communism: China, Chile, Czech Republic, Egypt, Hungary, India, Poland, and Russia. Since not even half of the emerging economies have had some form of increased central planning, it stands to reason that other economic systems have been more successful, on average, at developing nations out of poverty. However, each nation has a different set of circumstances and requires a different prescription for economic growth. I have argued, and continue to argue, that there is no one economic structure that is superior under all possible conditions. It is this thought that has led me to look at the conditions that led these states into socialism or a lesser centrally-planned model, how they fared under that system, and how they thrived after adopting more market-orientated policies.

I have already discussed the gradual changes taking place in China, and the difficulties faced by sudden policy shifts in Russia in the 1990s. I will complete this chapter by discussing the conditions of Chile and the Czech Republic, both of which went through what has since been defined as *Shock Therapy*.

---

[14] Shock Therapy – a sudden change from centrally planned, interventionist government policy into a free market driven economy with tightly controlled fiscal measures, and stable monetary policy – for a succinct and very basic description

Shock Therapy was applied when a nation faced oppressive levels of inflation, over-regulation, heavy government subsidies or ownership over the Commanding Heights of the economy, increasing levels of unemployment and poor fiscal policy, and protectionist trade policies. When Shock Therapy was applied, it immediately ended all price controls, withdrew subsidies from industry and privatized state-owned industry, while liberalizing trade over-night. I will further discuss a post-industrialized economy, Great Britain (U.K.), for a little more perspective on economic change and policy adoption. I'll finish the chapter by discussing Social Democracy and why socialism will not work in the developing world.

Chile

Chile is currently listed as one of the emerging economies in the world, even though it experienced a significant period of centralized planning from 1952 – 1973. The Great Depression began taking its toll on the Chilean economy in 1929 which to that point had been developing faster than all other nations in the region. Compared to other developing nations of the world at the time, it was also most likely hit the worst. Economic conditions were made even worse when, like many nations during the Great Depression, Chile adopted protectionist policies such as increased tariffs and quotas on imports. Its policies harmed its ability to trade freely among other nations in the world and its economy was adversely affected. Industries in Chile depended on many foreign imports for its production and were directly harmed by the new policies. Furthermore, World War II made imports even harder to attain among barely operating world markets and the Chilean economy further floundered. In 1932 the Chilean government began undertaking significant economic reforms that were ever-encroaching on the ability of its markets to operate freely. After the 1938 elections, more economic reforms were adopted and the state was well on its way to obtaining a large share of control over industry and centrally planned development was well underway.

In 1939 the government created the Corporación de Fomento de la Producción (CORFO). At first private industry was concerned over the creation of the CORFO, since its mandate was to create state-owned enterprises that directly competed with private industry, but eventually the public and private sectors operated with friendly relations. Unemployment was reduced throughout the 1940s and the economy improved. By 1950 the shortcomings of the government-owned industrialization started to become apparent, specifically in the agricultural sector that had largely been ignored by CORFO. [55]

Chile began experiencing large inflationary pressures from 1952-1955 with an annual rate reaching 86 percent. The government adopted countercyclical policies and under the direction of President Jorge Alessandri, who was elected in 1958, shifted toward a more market-orientated approach. The economy stagnated and disinflationary pressures took hold in 1960-61; Chile was not yet ready for market reforms. The government devalued its currency again in 1962, resumed restrictions on imports, and once again saw huge inflationary pressures that averaged 26.6 percent through his tenure. The GDP grew at an average rate of 3.7 percent and unemployment remained low at 5.2 percent. Even in the face of high inflation, it seemed the heavy government role in the economy was still necessary at that point in time [55].

Even in the presence of the inflationary pressures, import restrictions, and CORFO, government interventions proved relatively successful as long as the leadership sought macroeconomic equilibrium and acted accordingly. From 1964 through 1970, President Frei Montalva renewed and reinvigorated the role of the government in industry. Under his leadership the country began nationalizing large copper mines, banking, and other enterprises, while many private businesses were taken over by workers or political groups. The government was accelerating its drive toward socialism, not the free market, but with clear and feasible objectives. Under Montalva the nation's economy grew 4 percent per annum, unemployment only grew by 0.7 percentage points, and the inflation rate remained almost the same at 26.3 percent.

Conditions were not perfect, but the government had learned quite a lot about counterbalancing the economy through central means, and the free market was still operating to a large extent. The timing for change back toward a primarily free market approach was not quite perfect; stability under the then-current, centrally planned model was still necessary. Unfortunately, new elections were held in 1970 and a more socialist leaning leader was about to take office and upset the teetering balance between government and free markets.

The seeds of economic hardship were again sewn in 1970 when Salvador Allende was elected president. He ignored macroeconomic equilibrium and further nationalized the economy; while also politically distancing Chile from the United States, he *shocked* the economy with more socialist reforms. From 1970-1973 the economy grew at the meager rate of only 1.2 percent, saw lower unemployment of 4.7 percent, but reached an unprecedented inflationary rate of 294 percent. It did not take long for this to create unrest in the economy and eventually a military coup ended his reign. If the nation was not ready to convert back to a market-driven model in 1970, it certainly was after the tenure of Chile's new president.

Conditions were not good enough for a democratic leadership to fix Chile, but the introduction of a dictator seems to have been necessary for Chile in 1974. Military general Augusto Pinochet took the leadership role in 1974, and reigned until 1990. Even Friedrich Hayek advised his regime and readily admitted that a dictator is sometimes necessary through a transition period. In an interview in 1981 with the Chilean newspaper *El Mercurio*, Hayek said:

> [A]s long-term institutions, I am totally against dictatorships. But a dictatorship may be a necessary system for a transitional period. At times it is necessary for a country to have, for a time, some form or other of dictatorial power. As you will understand, it is possible for a dictator to govern in a liberal way. And it is also possible for a democracy to govern with a total lack of liberalism. Personally, I prefer a liberal dictator to democratic government lacking in liberalism. My personal impression. . . is that in Chile . . . we will witness a transition from a dictatorial government to a liberal government . . . during this transition it may be necessary to maintain certain dictatorial powers, not as something permanent, but as a temporary arrangement.

During this period, while under a dictatorial rule, Chile was transformed toward a market driven economy – though the 16 year conversion was not easy, nor was it peaceful. Pinochet is known to have slain his political rivals and thousands of other opponents within the population were killed or forced into exile. Still, many love Pinochet and regard him as a hero.

Under Pinochet the nation experienced slower growth than it had before Allende (2.9%), similar unemployment rates to what had occurred before Allende (18.1%), and worse inflation than the centrally-planned economy (79.9 %). The economy would eventually recover and develop into one of the world's emerging markets, but the path was long and arduous. The most important aspect of this recovery and conversion was likely stable future expectations. When the Chilean people and markets were able to adapt to the new economic situation, they were better able to make medium and long-term decisions for work and investment. Pinochet gave up the presidency in 1990 after losing a plebiscite in 1988. He remained Commander and Chief of the Chilean military until 1998 when he was appointed Senator for Life.

According to the CIA World Factbook, in 2013 Chile saw a national growth rate of about 4.4 percent, unemployment of 6 percent, and an inflation rate of 1.7 percent. It is possible Chile would have seen a natural economic correction from the Great Depression, but unlike the United States, Chile played almost no role in World War II; thus, there was no wartime industrialization to promise future economic improvement. Given the nation's set of circumstances, the only viable option appeared to be government action which set it on a road to recovery. It would have been interesting if Allende would never have taken office so we could have seen a natural conversion to markets; alas, it was not so.

Interventions from the 1940s through the 1960s played a very important role in setting the stage for a successful market economy after the difficult transition through the 1970s and 1980s. By building industry in the 1950s and 1960s and privatizing that industry in the 1970s and 1980s, the Chilean government sewed seeds of growth for the 1990s. Chile grew at an average rate of nearly 6% in the 1990s and that growth has not slowed much. Many will point to the booms and busts through the 40s, 50s, and 60s as proof that Chile's central plan was not working, but those ups and downs may have other origins as well. The natural business cycle that realizes a recession and boom every 7-10 years, or geopolitics and the fickle state of the entire world during the Cold War, could also be the reason for Chile's upturns and downturns at that time. One thing is clear, the industry-building the government did in the earlier decades, even with the inefficiencies produced by central government planning, proved helpful in the future decades. In the words of Chilean economist, Ricardo Ffrench-Davis:

> In the 1960s, excessive protection and administrative obstacles fostered inefficiencies, but greater real macroeconomic stability helped improve efficiency and keep more enterprises afloat. It concentrated effort on creating enterprises rather than on transferring existing assets and provided more predictable patterns of demand and more stable relative prices (which stimulated productive investment, given its irreversibility). Development was also more integrated, which offered more productive opportunities for broader sectors of society. This environment, despite numerous inefficiencies, explains the better performance of productivity in the 1960s, vis-á-vis the 1950s and the near match with potential productivity in the 1980s. [56]

While it is possible Chile may have seen a natural economic correction without intervention, it is also possible it would have continued to flounder. The necessity of the government intervention, and subsequent nationalization of the commanding heights, is likely the result of bad policy that made the Great Depression worse for the nation. Those same poor policies made government action necessary in Chile. The reasons for its economic crash are clear, but the effects of the interventions adopted by the Chilean government ultimately proved beneficial in the long term. Certainly the free market would have had a positive impact as well, but given the state of the world economy following World War II the Chilean economy could well have suffered for 40 years. At least with the government intervention it was able to soften the effects of its weak economy until 1970, even improving in some sectors. For Chile, the consequences of centrally planning its economy are clear, but at the time the decision to create CORFO was made it was a necessary action under the given set of conditions.

Czech Republic

The economy of what is today known as the Czech Republic[15] was booming after World War I: It had only taken until 1924 to reach prewar levels of industrialization, and by 1928 the unemployment rate was less than one percent. Of the working population 35 percent worked in agriculture, 34 percent in industry, and 31 percent in services. At the time this was an optimal division of the labor force. The Czechoslovak Republic, its name at the time, was the 10th largest industrial producer in the world [57].

When the Great Depression reached its peak in 1932-1933, industrial production had fallen by almost 40 percent; exports had virtually stopped and the Republic had gone from only

---

[15] For simplicity I am ignoring the Slovak region after the dissolution of Czechoslovakia and focusing on the Czech Republic. Before and after the dissolution, I will refer to Czechoslovakia simply as Czech.

38,000 unemployed in 1928 to over 1,000,000. Fascist rule had taken over Czech by the onset of the Second World War, and Czech industry was primarily converted to the production of war materials. Despite the allied bombing of Czech factories, the economy remained strong after World War II and poised for continued strong growth. Unfortunately the Russian leadership ordered Czech not to accept any loans or grants from the Marshall Plan and an era of communist rule began as Czech cozied up to the Soviet Union over western powers [57].

The socialization over the means of production began in 1948 as the government nationalized and adopted a policy of forced collectivism. Uniform Agricultural Cooperatives (JZD) were created where large and small farms alike were forced to relinquish their livestock, land, and capital equipment [57]. Throughout the period of socialist rule, however, Czech remained the premier producer of glass, textiles, and chemicals for the Soviet Union and its allies, as well as many other trading partners around the world. Bohemian Crystal was one of Czech's best-known exports. The government also nationalized and invested in the increased development of heavy industry.

Czech had enjoyed strong growth and the economy was booming in 1950 – even under communist rule industrial output had risen by almost 233% and unemployment had declined, most likely due to the communist consolidation of many industries. It appears not taking part in the Marshall plan did not hinder the economic possibilities for Czech, particularly because the country was aided by the Soviets, who wanted to maintain influence over the region. Central planning can only function for so long before inefficiencies manifest, however, and the Czech economy eventually began to cool in the early 1960s. This caused a wave of reformers to begin demanding political and economic change. The centrally planned reconstruction had served its purpose and the economy was ready to return to increased reliance on free market ideals.

The communist regime observed weaknesses that had been created by the socialist rule and began to soften communist policies in favor of longer-term, pro-growth strategies. Czech was attempting to adapt to the new economic conditions inside her borders, and market based reforms seemed relevant to the cause. Seeing its influence waning, Moscow decided to shore up Russia's support in the region. Facing resistance, fearing the loss of a key ally, and with the popular election of a reformer into office, the Soviets were concerned they might lose their grip over the Republic; they invaded in 1968.

This was a missed opportunity for the temporary adoption of centrally-planned reconstruction and economic rebuilding to prove successful. Instead, growth was thwarted by an oppressive communist regime attempting to perpetuate a long-term era of unsustainable, central-economic planning. Fifteen years of exceptional growth and the possibility of gradual change into free market capitalism were stopped, and the Czech economy grew slower than its potential. It did not matter how the economy recovered, via central planning or through unbridled markets, as long as the economy returned to long-term growth. Unfortunately, the Soviet government *shocked* Czech solidly into communist rule and ensured their return to growth and improved economic output would not happen for several more decades.

Czech was freed from Soviet rule during the Velvet Revolution in 1989, and in 1990 held its first democratic elections since 1946. Since then the nation has struggled to gain its economic footing but is considered one of the *Shock Therapy* success stories. Other nations who adopted *Shock Therapy* for economic reform were not so lucky and the policy is generally considered somewhat of a failure today. William Easterly wrote of *Shock Therapy*, *"Overnight transformation to a market economy had joined the list of failed utopian schemes."* [58]

Today Czech is listed as one of the OECD high income countries with per capita income of nearly $20,000 PPP (Purchasing Power Parity adjusted). According to the World Bank, the nation has experienced growth rates since 2004 that have ranged from as high as 7 percent to as low as -4.5 percent [59]. Unemployment levels have ranged from 8.3 percent in 2004 to only 4.4 percent in 2008. Throughout 2012-2014 unemployment has stood at nearly 7 percent, and we have seen a growth rate of around 3.3 percent. Czech is a strong, emerging economy.

Nationalizing the means of production in Czech did not prove fatal to its economy when it was timed properly and managed correctly, but that economy was likely going to maintain growth either way. Had the nation chosen western assistance over Soviet aid, it likely would have avoided the invasion in 1968 and the Velvet Revolution may never have been necessary. In this case one may conclude that, in the 1940s and not knowing what the future might hold, either decision would have worked to develop the Czech economy after World War II. As long as the conversion back toward capitalist mechanisms is properly timed, only the conditions of the economy dictate what form of political-economy is adopted for the short term.

United Kingdom
Of the nations in the world that attempted socialist policies or government ownership over the means of production, we must also include, perhaps most surprisingly, the United Kingdom

(U.K.). The U.K. emerged from World War I with a very weak economy and it struggled even more through World War II. The U.K. was unique among industrialized economies in that after being ravaged by two world wars, its infrastructure and industrial base was teetering on complete failure. Its industrial base was probably as close as any industrialized nation can fall before reaching the point of complete disrepair. The great nation had simply fallen too far to get up without major policy revision and outside assistance. In 1945 the Labor party gained a majority in the leadership and socialized the means of production over the coal, iron, steel, railroad, utilities, and international telecommunications industries, and began centrally planning their economy [60].

Unemployment following World War I jumped dramatically in the U.K. It reached 16.9% in 1921, dropped and hovered between 10 and 14% throughout the 1920s and increased all the way to 22.1% in 1932. The Great Depression did not do the U.K. any favors with unemployment bouncing about between 16% and 22.1% throughout the 1930s. World War II ensured unemployment would drop as men went off to serve the nation in combat, but that did not provide any sort of promise for the nation after the war. After Britain's nationalization over the commanding heights of the economy, unemployment sank and stayed between 1.3% and 3.8% from 1945 to 1974. Unemployment is typically a good measure of economic well-being, but, as we shall see in this case, it can also bias our evaluation [61].

When industries are nationalized it is not difficult to keep unemployment relatively low, since one mandate a government might have is to keep as many people employed as it can. So it is important to look at other measures. According to the Bank of

England, the annual growth rate for the U.K. was -10.14% in 1921 [16]. By 1922 it had completely turned around, achieving an impressive rate of 6.25%. Growth remained positive the rest of the decade except in 1926. The Great Depression saw the economy stagnate somewhat, but still the U.K. maintained mostly positive growth rates, ranging from -4.97% in 1931 to a maximum of 6.21% in 1934. With wartime production the economy grew even faster in 1940, at an annual rate of 11.29%. However, after sustaining repeated bombardment and with its wartime debt mounting, the economy began to shrink, sinking to an annual growth rate similar to that of the Great Depression at -4.85% in 1944. In 1945 growth was even more dismal [16].

After nationalization over the means of production, the economy finally saw improvement, and from 1948 through 1974 growth averaged 2.75%. On the surface, even the growth rates seem to support an argument in favor of the state controlling the Commanding Heights, perhaps even to the extent that the state might have weathered the new problems in 1974. Stable growth and low unemployment are both desirable, but there is one more measure that must be considered before we can draw a conclusion on the state of the British economy.

When governments begin propping up industries within their borders, those industries are no longer subject to market forces, but they are subject to political pressures. If markets go down, the government uses tax money to subsidize failing industries. If markets improve, governments might politicize their success, or expand nationalization to include even more industries. These sorts of reactions make state ownership over the means of production a precarious beast. In 1945 it might have been necessary to socialize the means of production, and through 1968 that socialization may have stabilized the economy, helped with employment, and maintained a positive growth rate. Unfortunately, government spending had been expanding to unsustainable levels, and to fund that spending the top marginal income tax rate reached 83% by 1974. Add in another 15% for unearned income (similar to a capital gains tax) and people could have been taxed all the way up to as much as 98% [60] of their income [62]! Government ownership over the Commanding Heights had outlived its usefulness, conditions had changed, and reform was necessary.

Inflation began to take hold in 1969 with a rate of 5.4%. A single outlying data-point would not be that concerning, but just two years before the inflation rate was a normal 2.5%. That increased in 1968 to 4.7%, continued rising after 1969, and finally reached its apogee of 24% in 1975. From 1974 through 1982 the average inflation rate was 14.32%. Something that cost $3.50 in 1974 would have cost $11.59 by the beginning of 1983[16].

Workers were unhappy with stagnant wages, high inflation, and recent losses to some of their rights to strike or display their displeasure with the leadership and the economy. In 1972 coal workers demanded, and the government capitulated, a 22% increase to their wages. Further folly occurred in 1973 and 1974 when the coal miners banned overtime, slowing output and eventually ending production completely. The government instituted a three-day workweek and nationalized even more industry, including Rolls-Royce, and largely subsidized other heavy industry. Markets were malfunctioning, prices were rising, tax revenues were falling, unions were slowing or stopping production, and the British economy was stumbling.

---

[16] I used $3.50 because that is roughly the price of gasoline today in the United States. – Imagine paying $11.59 per gallon!

Further nationalization was not the answer, even if it had worked throughout the 1950s and 1960s. Market-orientated reforms were the prescription the U.K. needed, not more socialism.

It was not until Margaret Thatcher was elected in 1975 that the government finally started debating the reverse of the socialist policies. In 1979 Thatcher was elected Prime Minister in the national election and was finally able to fully turn national policies toward growth. As the markets floundered following World War II, socialist policies brought the U.K. through a tough time and built the systems necessary for the free-market to function successfully. Government intervention had worked to stabilize a floundering economy after World War II, but those policies had become obsolete by the middle of the 1960s. Only after the government finally began decreasing taxes back to sustainable levels, privatizing the previous Commanding Heights industries, and adopting a more monetarist view over the fiscal approach to their problems, did the economy begin its decade-long march back toward a long-run, sustainable level of output.

The socialist policies had served their purpose, and after too many years of socialist interventionism it was time for a market-led approach to Britain's economic ails. Today the United Kingdom has a strong, market-driven economy with some socialist programs such as national education and healthcare. The mixed economy approach is working under the current set of conditions, but the future may change the circumstances and require even greater change toward or away from free market policies.

Social Democracy

Socialism (Democratic Socialism) is not always as evil as it is sometimes portrayed. Great Britain, for example, achieved a significant level of socialism throughout the 20th century and it did so via the democratic process. France, Denmark, Norway, Sweden, and other countries have all adopted many socialist policies. Whether a particular culture wants nationalized healthcare or public education, minimum wages or maximum differential wage controls, mandated vacation or fewer hours per work week, sometimes socialized policies can work. Since it comes into existence through either the democratic process or by the demand of a popular protest movement, it can often be adapted as conditions permit.

Social conditions often permit popular socialized programs. Universal primary and secondary education, for example, are typically desired among the people of every nation. An educated population benefits society, private business, and government alike. A functioning infrastructure is also important and usually supported among the population. Public investment into infrastructure, such as highways, sanitation, seaports, airports, etc., provides avenues for trade in world markets and inlets for local investment. Goods can move around more freely and everyone in the nation benefits. Many social programs eventually enjoy popular support, become the norm, and even lose their stigma with time[17].

No matter what change occurs, social adaptation takes time. Czech, Poland, Chile, etc, have all endured *Shock Therapy*, but still took more than a decade to move toward their path of being defined as emerging economies. China moved glacially away

---

[17] Social Security in the U.S. is sometimes considered the third rail of politics. If it cannot be fixed then politicians are afraid to touch the program. The system itself enjoys wide-reaching support and its repair, not its dissolution, is the popular concern among the public. Highways, a standing military, sanitation, and clean water are other popular, socially provided goods – though there are many more.

from pure communism and is only now permitting greater market reforms. Russia endured 15 years of slow growth and is now experiencing pressure from Cold War mentalities and those who "remember a better time." Great Britain shifted from its Commanding Heights approach in 1979, and over the course of more than a decade it experienced slow growth and hardship before real improvement was realized.

Where markets are already functioning, where government intervention is minimal, where market ideals are not abusing society or nature, or where suspension of market systems might be damaging, those conditions are perfect for the continued operation of successful free markets and capitalism. Where markets can be encouraged, where government can sow the seeds to future growth, where temporary suspension of free market ideals can lead to a better future, those conditions might be perfect for successful temporary socialism or permanent socialist policies. When conditions exist in which the economy is growing and people are happy, the government is not needed. When shortcomings of government or markets become evident, change is necessary. An infinite number of combinations exist for the above conditions, and there are an immense number of conditions that have been ignored. Where conditions permit an action, or require a change, commit to the action and commit to the change, but always ignore an entrenched ideology. There is nothing more destructive than an unwillingness to adapt; unwillingness to adapt is usually borne by a closed mind.

Why Not Short Term Socialism to Solve Poverty?
One thing Czech, Chile, and U.K. all had in common when they adopted centrally-planned models was an already existing industrial and tax base, even if it was malfunctioning at the time.

Realistically, most of the developing nations of the world do not have the funding available to invest in industry or capital equipment; their industrial base is weak or nonexistent, and the tax base is too poor to tax. Often they may not even have the funds to pay for proper court systems and judges. Certainly they have trouble paying local police and bailiffs to protect courts and ensure rulings are enforced. If the population has enough money or if outside influences are willing to make loans or invest, then markets work efficiently to push an economy forward and into growth. When populations do not have money and FDI (Foreign Direct Investment) is not readily available, but governments have funding or can acquire the helpful loans, then socialist policy works in the short-term. Once inefficiencies become evident it is then necessary to convert to a market-driven economy.

By the point of conversion from socialism to free markets, investment by governments into infrastructure and industry could already have positioned an economy to better utilize market structures and mechanisms. Due to government investment, they will have the equipment, tools, buildings, and other capital necessary to privatize and retool if necessary. After World War II, for example, many wartime factories in the United States were converted to produce other products. Unfortunately, the developing world has neither the advantage of a wealthy or even a middle-class population, nor money in government coffers for public investment. In the absence of both, they are left with little choice except to rely on outside influences to develop from extreme poverty, and aid becomes essential.

Communism has largely disappeared from our world, so there is no need for any particular case study on communist nations (though we certainly should never forget our history lest we are doomed to its repeat). It is important to note, however, that in many of the nations where communism rose to power it was rather similar to another type of *Shock Therapy*. Where markets were suffering and the economy faced many similarities to those above, government takeover seemed like a legitimate idea. That takeover usually stabilized the economy for a short period before it too became too cumbersome, and the need for new change was illuminated. Any sudden change can lead to short-term stability from the new hope it creates, or abrupt upheaval from the uncertainty it spawns. The problem is that populations rarely have the patience to travel the long road to economic adjustment and recovery. The road is often a decade or more of winding, slow, growth as markets and populations adjust to new changes – capitalist, socialist, or otherwise.

Sudden changes toward (or away from) either type of economy, centrally planned or market driven, are harmful to an economy for years or even decades. We may desire more free markets in our world, and in the long-run we will likely reach that goal. However, the people of each nation and the conditions they face will be the most important aspect of any change. If they do not trust in an improved future outlook, they will demand change. When change occurs too frequently, the nation will suffer from uncertainty and they will sink into a poverty trap.

Part 3: Poverty and Solutions

Chapter 6: Aid, Nations, and Dependence

*"... our aim in founding the State was not the disproportionate
happiness of any one class, but the greatest happiness of the
whole; we thought that in a State which is ordered with a view to
the good of the whole we should be most likely to find justice,
and in the ill-ordered State injustice: and, having found them,
we might then decide which of the two is happier."*

– Plato

Why Nations Fail

Nations fail for myriad reasons. In the former Soviet Union we
know it was poor central planning and a lack of proper
incentives for the industrial workers to produce and the
agricultural sector to grow. International seclusion from trade
and markets did not help either. In South America we are well
aware that it is poor governance inspired by poor institutions and
a lack of private property rights that slows the economy. In the
far-east it is clearly brutal, dictatorial, and perceived omniscience
that is keeping North Korea in abject poverty. Africa and south
Asia have their own set of problems, many shared with other
impoverished regions of the world.

The conditions of each part of the world are surely similar, even
sharing many of the same problems which often stem from the
same source (such as private property rights, bad governance, or
poor institutions). Each region has its own major concerns,
however; and as I hope you have begun to learn by now that all
conditions require a different prescription for economic
development. Many parts of the world presently suffer not only
from corruption, but still from the negative economic impact due
to a history colored by colonialism. They suffer from a past

diseased by slavery, economic pillaging, and poor colonial governance [63].

Slavery has had dire economic consequences on all involved in the trade. There is much research on the economies where slaves were extracted and where they were sold or used as capital [64]. Institutions, governance, and long-term growth paths all deteriorated in the presence of the slave trade. Nations where slaves were extracted experienced ethnic fragmentation, internal conflicts between communities, and the general weakening of governments and nations throughout the colonial period. The negative effects were not limited to the states that sold slaves, but also the states that utilized slave labor. Nations that never turned to slave labor, or did on a relatively limited basis, developed far more equal societies, universal suffrage, property rights, etc. Engerman and Sokoloff write,

> ...great equality or homogeneity among the population led, over time, to more democratic political institutions, to more investment in public goods and infrastructure, and to institutions that offered relatively broad access to economic opportunities. In contrast, where there was extreme inequality, as in most of the societies of the Americas, political institutions were less democratic, investments in public goods and infrastructure were more limited, and the institutions that evolved tended to provide highly unbalanced access to economic opportunities and thereby greatly advantaged the elite. [64]

This inequality, driven by short-term institutions or poor economic policies, did not promote growth. The nations that opted for more slave labor also unwittingly opted for decreased future wealth prospects.

As nations colonized other portions of the world, they often instituted a short-term government in order to extract as much wealth as possible before abandoning distant lands. Sadly, nations did not limit themselves to natural resources alone, taking humans as slave labor in addition to other forms of capital and wealth. The Conquistadors took ignominious levels of gold and silver from South America; the British imposed their odious rule to acquire anything they desired from East Asia and Africa; the French and Portuguese exploited large swaths of Africa and Latin America. Far too many colonial powers adopted similar ruinous programs of short term exploitation all over the globe. All of the European powers did nothing less than pillage the entire planet for their own, short-term gain. Great empires ranging from the Incan to the Chinese were not immune.

As Europeans colonized many parts of the world, they implemented policies that exploited or enslaved local labor and then shipped the riches back to their homelands. They had little interest in continued growth and governance in the regions they were exploiting – particularly in Africa – only getting rich as quickly as possible and then moving on to the next colony. They had no desire and thus no reason to look to the future of their colonies or the local peoples; they were simply taking as much as they could as quickly as they could. Unless there was an opportunity for long-term extraction of some natural resource, many distant colonies were never meant to be permanent.

In the absence of wealth that could be extracted, European settlers often sought other avenues to riches. South of the mainland of North America, soils were rich in nutrients and perfectly suited for the growth of sugar, for example. The elites of Brazil enslaved the local populations and shipped in millions of slaves from Africa in order to farm their plantations. Since there was not any gold in North America on the east coast to mine and the local peoples were more organized and homogenous, other production had to be considered. North America could not be exploited in the same way other portions of the world had been, and the Europeans had to change their practices.

North American settlers were forced to adopt a new long-term model for colonization instead of the traditional pillage, plunder, and leave model they had been accustomed too; stronger governance and accountability was required. To be successful the colonists would need to plan long-term, renewable investments and find a new way to exploit the local geography to their advantage instead of the local tribes. Private property titles were instituted, though usually through common means rather than explicitly legal systems, suffrage became more common, communities invested in schools and infrastructure, and North American societies enjoyed a generally more equal society. They realized stronger growth and more economic stability. Some investors began farming large plantations in the south while others developed industries in the north. Of course, the institution of slavery, mostly imported from overseas, was still prevalent, unfortunately.

Strong institutions and rule of law are among the most important factors for economic growth [65]. Logical, understandable laws and legal institutions began in North America as early as Jamestown. The Jamestown settlers understood that they would be there for a long time, and after more than 440 settlers out of 500 starved to death in 1609, it became clear they needed a longer term plan. Attempting to abandon the settlement in the summer of 1610, the settlers were turned back by a supply fleet led by their new governor, Thomas West, 3rd Baron De La Warr.

De La Warr had come with new supplies and several different types of tobacco seeds with plans to plant a new cash crop for the colony. Instead of exploiting the colony for non-renewable natural resources and then leaving, the colony began growing tobacco for trade and became self-sufficient. Since tobacco was a renewable resource, it could be exploited indefinitely. Better governance and stable institutions lead to a stronger, permanent colony.

Uncertainty is the best way to destroy an economy. After uncertainty it is poor institutions that lead to bad governance. Since many natural resources had been mined to depletion during colonialism, and without the technology to develop more difficult-to-obtain supplies, local populations lacked tradable goods when the Europeans abandoned their colonies. A power vacuum, ripe for authoritarianism, was all that remained after the Europeans left. With unpredictable rules and laws, weak property rights, and few options for trade, former European colonies were left to flounder – often under the oppressive nature of a capricious dictator. Worse, natural boundaries between nations, typically emerging from ethnic division or cultural differences, were ignored by the Europeans. Governments that formed later were weakened as a result of the arbitrary nature of national division done by leaders at the Berlin Conference. Smaller ethnic groups were often under-represented, and human rights were easily abused – a state not uncommon even today. Nations failed then and struggle now as a result of so many problems created from the destructive period of colonialism.

Investment and Incentives

Economics is the study of incentives. Without proper incentives, no invention and certainly no innovation would ever be created or adopted. I often quip that during college I was motivated by laziness, since I went to college hoping to avoid a manual labor job – I worked selling tires early in my college years, a dirty, nasty job to be sure but not incredibly physically demanding or difficult. I could not have known then that using my brain is still exhausting, but a lot more fun. Nevertheless, incentives matter. Whether people want more money, more fun, more free-time, more recognition, etc, something motivates people to do whatever it is they do. Governments, like people, also respond to incentives. The advanced nations of the world have very little incentive, for example, to create trade relations with smaller, less developed or bottom billion countries for the most part.

It is important to realize that governments create trade agreements, but it is corporations and entrepreneurs who act on those agreements and decide whether to invest in particular regions in the world. Unfortunately, there is very little economic incentive to invest in the world's developing nations, particularly for those corporations already successfully operating elsewhere. When populations are small or sickly, people are unemployed or unskilled, governments are corrupt or unstable, the rule of law is weak or nonexistent, and the risk to investments is very high, then investors will seek other vehicles for profit in safer regions of the world. In more volatile parts of the world, even ignoring the presence of internal threats and civil unrest, governments must also worry about unstable neighbors invading. When one country invades another, uncertainty is created and economies are destroyed – even when the U.N. intervenes quickly.

In such dubious geopolitical environments, more stable governments have difficulty making or enforcing trade agreements with unstable or impoverished nations; corporations often seek easier, more secure options even when favorable trade agreements have been signed. As failed states are taken over by popular leaders who seem to inevitably become dictators until ousted, it is very difficult to make lasting agreements or create safe harbors for investment funds or capital. Under such conditions the opportunity cost of investment is simply too high for anyone looking to build or expand new business. Even when trade is possible and barriers are removed, it is often still unprofitable for investors after they account for the greater risks involved. Entrepreneurs and CEOs, just like governments and voters, must also take circumstances into account when making business decisions.

Earlier in this book it was concluded that war is a root cause leading to inflationary policies; war is also a major cause which can lead to almost all other economic ruin and hardship – one side or the other might eventually win, but the citizens of the countries involved always lose since capital in these nations will be damaged, misused or destroyed. Since trade agreements among a few stable nations are far easier to accomplish than trade agreements with many volatile states, governments focus where their respective corporations will get the most benefit, which by proxy maximizes the benefits of their citizens. They do not have much incentive to focus elsewhere (these could include reasons of national security, as discussed earlier). Even when an effort is made to promote trade in the developing world, governments are often led to provide incentives to corporations to invest in the poverty effected regions. Without strong, direct incentives businesses face risks that are too great for investment. By pushing foreign investment incentives programs, politicians face domestic political pressure – with good reason – to avoid placing incentives to begin with. Citizens do not like when business is outsourced, so incentives remain unpopular. Voters like even less when their tax dollars are spent abroad when they know there are valid investments being overlooked at home. Even when foreign aid and spending is in their best interest, e.g., reducing the price of consumer goods, convincing one's constituents can be difficult.

Certain nations, like India and China, provide an abundance of cheap labor, an obvious natural advantage, and a relatively stable government structure with clear rules. Other impoverished nations do not have either of those particular advantages. In the absence of large populations and in the presence of volatility, outside corporations do not always have an obvious reason to invest; in fact they have clear reasons not too. Surely the whole of Africa would fill the need for cheap, abundant labor, but there are between 54 and 56 nations in Africa at any particular point in time. More importantly, bottom billion nations often do not guarantee private property rights and they frequently suffer coups d'état or war with neighboring states. Investors could have their inventories and operations seized by the government or destroyed by warlords; they could lose their investment capital or be bankrupted without legal recourse. In such an uncertain environment, not only do international business people have no incentive to invest, they often face a negative incentive and have valid reasons *not* to invest.

The advanced economies of the world already have successful trade relations with many other nations, though they always seek better agreements or less expensive and more efficient forms of output. The result is that until the underdeveloped world proves able to safely and stably fill the needs of foreign investors, it will be largely avoided. The perception of instability in the underdeveloped world sows the seeds for real instability, creating a paradox of needing stability to have stability. Without growth of industry in a nation to help mass produce and export goods, the advantage of international trade is foregone and the advanced nations of the world can continue to ignore the large swath of the world in perpetual poverty – outside of foreign aid and assistance, that is.

Aid Gone Wrong

The peoples of the developing world lack necessary skills, equipment, connections, and finances to develop their way out of poverty. They may lack any combination of

1. Knowledge, education, skills or training to become entrepreneurs, build capital equipment, or develop natural resources.
2. Connections to developers, government officials, or bankers in the developed nations.
3. Money to invest, invent, or innovate.
4. Availability of local banks to acquire loanable funds to acquire capital for increased and improved production.

Aid done incorrectly creates an entirely new problem, however. When markets do finally begin to emerge within a bottom billion economy, they are often destroyed by outside interference. The destruction created by poor aid mechanisms does not mean we should stop our aid programs, but it does mean our aid programs need retooling. It took the world roughly 50 years to come to that conclusion, and in many places today aid is being distributed in a far different way. However, in many places outside interference is still destroying local markets. It happens like this:

A local farmer grows some rice to sell or trade to other local people in the community. The community would happily purchase the rice from the farmer, providing him much needed supplies, labor, or other tradable goods that they had produced in exchange. This market activity would improve the farmer and his family's life, that of the people he had employed, and those with whom he traded. Through the trading activities, the people the farmer traded with would also be able to conduct further trade, employ workers, and expand their market activities as well. Instead of paying, however, the local population goes to the local food bank and collects free rice from an international aid organization, since *free* is better than *not-free*. The local farmer cannot sell his rice at any price and begins giving his rice away for free or possibly destroying it. This further harms the market and other farmers facing the same competition with the international aid organization. The market as a whole begins to fail as prices approach zero and incentives to produce disappear. Facing no incentive to produce rice in the next rice season, the farmer does not grow any rice; after all, the local food bank will feed him and his family for free and without his labor. Those the farmer would have employed no longer have jobs and are also unable to invest to improve their own families' lives. The standard of living begins to decrease, and the people become dependent on outside aid.

Ironically, the aid can harm the people it was meant to assist when it destroys the markets where it ignores existing price and supply structures. As decades pass, knowledge and skills normally passed from grandfather to grandson have been lost or severely degraded. In the 21st century those would-be farmers no longer know how to farm efficiently, and broken markets have emerged. The example is about farming, but the problem permeates all aspects of many of these societies. Skills can be lost in farming, teaching, building, mechanical knowledge, and more. Worse, in many places skills are even lost in governing, giving rise to another of the poverty traps.

The people of developing nations can barter, build, and invest, but often that only helps maintain the status quo; they do not have the funds to invest in capital intensive projects and they are only able to trade locally. Certainly local business people can open a storefront, but who would purchase their items in a world where everyone is poor and few people have anything of value to trade? Furthermore, once a business is successful in an environment of uncertain private property rights, there is no guarantee the owner will be able to retain the business if the government or a corrupt official decides to take it from them. Even bartering is sometimes hindered since many among these nations are also without skill or training to produce tradable goods. In the developing world people lack the education, banking, and private property institutions that would help them develop effective markets to help them escape their perpetual state of poverty.

Why Aid Is not Working

It is difficult to convince some people and organizations that aid is bad, largely because much aid is not bad. It is true, however, that aid which is meant to help can often have the exact opposite effect. It is counterintuitive to consider that giving food or money can actually have deleterious consequences on the economy where the aid is provided and to those living in poverty. There has been much literature on how aid helps or harms, but probably the most persuasive evidence is presented in the book *Dead Aid*, by Dambisa Moyo [66]. Moyo lays out essentially four reasons why aid can actually be bad for an economy. He does not claim that aid should stop entirely, only that the methods for how it is implemented need to be rethought.

Monetary aid can have deleterious effects on the incentives leaders face and can lead to the corruption of otherwise effective leadership. Corruption is a well-known problem in the developing world. As money flows in from the industrialized nations' governments, NGO's, and philanthropists, much is simply deposited back in western banks by the officials in control and never invested in the actual economy where it was intended. The corrupt politicians get richer while their people continue to suffer. Unfortunately, the people do not have a direct, observable consequence from this redirection of aid funds and therefore rarely, if ever, demand accountability from these same politicians and leaders. Simply put, the people do not know the aid exists and they are unaware that it has been corruptly redirected.

Additionally, many aid agencies do not measure the effectiveness of their agency by the efficiency of their aid. Often western aid agencies efforts are measured simply by the gross quantity of aid they provide [58]. Furthermore, as less monetary aid than was provided actually makes it to the populations for which it was intended, western agencies often increase the aid they provide and call it successful aid funding. The corrupt officials are perfectly aware that more theft means more aid, and therefore continue taking portions of the aid as it is distributed. More aid often means more corruption and a cycle of continued poverty.

Further complicating the aid problem, corrupt leaders find ways to retain their offices against the best interests of their constituencies. They may offer incentives – like effective tax rates of zero percent – to their electorate and can even be popular among their countrymen. Rather than becoming civil statesmen, they seemingly help their impoverished people by reducing taxes and relying greatly on ostensibly interminable aid. Rather than utilizing the aid to invest in basic infrastructure like roads, schools, hospitals, or sanitation, they redirect the funds to supplement their own lavish lifestyles. The citizens of the nations where the tax rate is essentially zero are not paying for the expected government services; therefore, they rarely demand their government officials become more accountable. Since the corrupt officials retain office and the citizens do not revolt, the aid continues – ineffectively.

Endlessly ignoring the necessary improvements and investment they could make within their borders, politicians grow wealthy and retain power. *Forbes* magazine reports there are 29 African billionaires, up from 20 just one year ago. One should not automatically assume these billionaires are corrupt; perhaps they are just good business people with good intentions and great entrepreneurial skills, but that is a 45% increase in the number of billionaires on the poorest continent in the world. The legitimacy of much of that wealth should certainly be scrutinized. Not even the richest nations on Earth have seen such a drastic increase in the number of billionaires. The increase would be laughable if it were not so disturbing. Whether we define this as bad leadership or corruption at the highest levels, the aid is not accomplishing what it was intended and it is not flowing to its intended targets. As the peoples of these nations cry out for help from the wealthier nations across the globe, and the corrupt officials appear successful in acquiring foreign aid for their people, perpetual dependence on foreign aid is realized to the increased detriment of the neediest societies.

Giving money to impoverished nations can also encourage inflation; thus, the minute wealth of the poorest individuals that aid is intended to help is diminished. As money flows into a poor nation, be it from foreign governments, private donors or aid agencies, it increases the demand within the economy where the aid is spent. Perhaps the aid leads to a corrupt official purchasing a car and some new clothing, the money flows downward through the tiers of society and new demand is created. New demand would normally have a positive effect in an economy, driving new investment and jobs. In an impoverished nation, however, it can have dire consequences. Often the poorest nations on earth have not made agreements for freer trade with each other or with western nations. With a shortage of trade options, aid puts otherwise absent pressures on the supplies of consumer goods. New money begins chasing fewer scarce goods and prices rise in the already poor society.

Increasing demand too quickly can mean exacerbating the blight of the poor. A large influx of money can increase demand and reduce the availability of already limited inventories for consumer goods. Limited inventory translates to reduced supply and upward pressure on prices. Paul Collier writes, "*in a poor environment, there are not any more cars, there are not any more clothes, so with increased demand prices go up,*" and where else would they go? The pricing mechanism redirects resources to their most valued use, and the wealthier individuals in any society will still be free to purchase higher priced goods. Since supplies are limited and not replaced quickly, prices rise, and the poorest in our world are left without access to otherwise more affordable consumer goods.

In an environment with higher prices, the local population is forced to divest what little savings it has managed to acquire in order to make normal consumer purchases. Since domestic savings decrease, local bank reserves fall – assuming there are local banks and that the poor have bank accounts – interest rates rise and domestic investment within the economy declines. When businesses are unable or choose not to invest, no jobs are created, markets slow or cease to operate, and the poor remain poor or get poorer. The more likely scenario is that the poor simply spend what little money they had squirreled away, and they are unable to invest in new activities, since few who are living in abject poverty even retain a bank account. They are very likely to live day to day wondering where their next meal will come from and have no savings to divest. Though new demand has placed more money into the economy, the poorest people are worse off than they were before since their cost of living increased, their wages remained constant, and their savings, if they had any, fell.

While aid from abroad can cause the weakening of a nation's currency, large inflows of cash can also lead to the opposite, yet equally harmful, condition known as "Dutch Disease." A foreign nation's currency is not typically accepted for domestic trade, so through exchange markets local money must first be acquired. To acquire local money, foreign aid agencies must first convert their currencies, via the foreign exchange currency market, into the local currency. This means a lot of foreign aid money is supplied to the foreign exchange markets and demand for the currency they desire rises. When demand rises, the value of the foreign currency rises as well and Dutch Disease is born.

Typically Dutch Disease is made real when reserves of natural resources are discovered and large amounts of financial capital flow in from abroad. The flow can be in the form of foreign aid or by a change in foreign direct investment. Foreign money purchases the host nation's domestic currency, decreasing its supply on the foreign exchange, and then is immediately invested in the development of resources inside the host country. As resources are built and developed inside the host country, the repatriation of its currency occurs very quickly. The exchange rate changes faster than the repatriated money can propagate through the population, and the people are not able to adapt. Exports decline as the exchange rate rises, and though the host nation's currency is now more valuable, imports do not increase fast enough to mitigate the effects of the change in exchange rates. As exports decline and local exporters halt production, supplies decrease. As more money and increased demand chases fewer goods with decreased supply, the economy experiences inflationary pressures, increasing unemployment, and decreasing investment. Dutch Disease is realized, and the economy the investment was intended to benefit is actually harmed.

Dutch Disease can be difficult to grasp, so consider the following example from your personal perspective:

> You hope to purchase a Sudanese, hand-made shirt. To do so, you first need to purchase Sudanese pounds (SDG) with your dollars. Perhaps the shirt costs 100 SDG, and the exchange of dollars to SDG is $1.00 per 5 SDG. This means the Sudanese shirt will cost $20.00 after the monetary conversion. However, what happens to your purchasing decision if just before your purchase the IMF decides to inject millions of dollars of aid into the Sudanese economy through corporations hoping to develop new reserves of recently discovered oil? They first purchase the SDG with dollars, and the exchange rate rises. The increased demand for SDGs might cause the exchange rate to change from $1.00 per 5 SDG to

$1.00 per 4 SDG instead. The price of your Sudanese shirt would then become $25. Maybe at $25 you decide not to purchase the shirt after all, and as Sudanese shirt exports fall, Sudanese shirt makers lose their jobs or go out of business.

It is not just the shirt market in the above example where exports fall after the change in the exchange rate. Exports fall across the entire Sudanese economy. When exports fall, businesses in Sudan no longer need as many employees, and they lay off workers. When workers are laid off, demand in the Sudanese economy declines and more businesses decide to cut expenses.

Prices for citizens inside Sudan would change too; imports would actually become less expensive. Unfortunately, the Sudanese citizens are now unemployed and cannot purchase the imports, even though they are cheaper. Since they no longer have a professional vocation to pay their bills and buy goods and services, the Sudanese become poorer than they would have been without the aid. Less money is spent inside Sudan, both domestically and from abroad, and revenues across the country decrease. Since profits are decreasing across the Sudanese economy, investment seems risky and new businesses decide not to open while existing businesses either stop expansion or close altogether. Displaced workers and previous business owners may attempt to gain employment in the Sudanese oil fields, further decreasing business activity and pressuring the economy even further. The population becomes dependent on imports and aid and once the oil dries up the foreign investors leave. Without oil jobs to employ the Sudanese people, they are left unemployed in an economy where the people cannot afford to import goods and are no longer producing exports. Import businesses fail, and a shortage of capital creates an environment of slow growth and poverty.

Aid can harm existing markets, destroy local businesses, eliminate jobs, and increase unemployment in other ways as well. Some aid comes in the form of free agricultural products or capital goods. Under some circumstances free goods and services can be an excellent stop-gap measure to ensure continuity of society and future growth – for example after a major weather, geopolitical, or geological event. The stop-gap measure would be useful in the previous example after the oil dries up as well, assuming the leaders did not already take measures during the oil boom to guarantee a better future for their nation. However, permanent recurring free goods and services have a toxic effect on existing local markets. Local farmers may sell food at the local markets; free food from a "competing" aid organization is far more appealing to the local population than food that is not free, and they substitute in favor of free food as discussed before.

Aid may be necessary, but sometimes the affect can be disastrous. Providing cash to politicians who are in charge of an impoverished nation can take away their incentive to invest in their economy and potentially harm natural price mechanisms. Those same politicians may implement an effective tax rate of zero; those who they rule may never insist on change, unknowingly bolstering their continued existence in perpetual poverty. Providing free food or capital goods will create competition for local businesses and possibly make them unable to compete. Free food and capital goods provided to a nation may kill fledgling markets that were already developing. Economies that are already experiencing large amounts of inflation do not need large injections of cash. In this situation, cash is exactly the opposite of what they need. If a country's currency is increasingly more valuable while floating against an outside currency, then increasing the value of that currency may also be harmful. Exports can help bring a nation out of poverty, so making that nation's goods more expensive is not a solution.

Why Nations Cannot Grow

Many papers and books have been written on the topic of international development and poverty. Paul Collier is among the most influential and he identified four major reasons nations remain impoverished. Dr. Collier refers to the four factors that keep nations from developing as development traps [67]. The four development traps are the conflict trap, natural resources trap, landlocked trap, and bad governance trap. Without first addressing these four problems, he claims, nations will not move from poverty into abundance and therefore will remain trapped in a perpetual state of poverty.

The conflict trap occurs for impoverished nations far too frequently. Even when good politicians enter the leadership, or when idealistic revolutionaries are successful in taking control of the government and have truly good intentions, they can be inhibited by the existing level of poverty in their nation. They may lack access to outside markets, money for development, or skills to operate the government effectively. Impoverished nations often suffer from bad relations with the neighboring governments who sometimes invade to settle old debts or vendettas. Some developing countries' governments are too young to have established strong ties to more wealthy states and have trouble when they seek assistance from without. Tensions rise within their borders and they are at constant risk from another internal uprising. Nations that have suffered a recent civil war have about a 50% chance of falling back into conflict again within 10 years [67]. Furthermore, at any given 5-year interval, bottom billion nations have about a 14% chance of falling into civil war. [67]. There is hope, however, since economic growth can actually decrease the risk from conflict. Every 1% increase to a poor nation's growth rate decreases its chance of falling into war by about 1% [67].

The natural resources trap is a bit less intuitive. If a nation has many natural resources, like the United States, then it should surely find growth an easy accomplishment. But then there are other nations, like Hong Kong, that have few or no natural resources and still find a seemingly easy path to wealth. The natural resource trap stems from deeper systemic problems in a nation. There are not one but two natural resources traps: abundant resources like diamonds or oil, or too few resources to export. Conflict can arise for control over resources, civil war or invasion, or populations can become dependent on their exportation as they are depleted. Dutch Disease can be realized when the population is suddenly enriched by an influx of financial capital. Worse, when labor is repurposed toward mining or resource exploitation, then other sectors' development may be completely ignored. When resource reservoirs run dry, the economies of developing nations frequently do not have the institutions in place to weather the weakened state of the economy. Poverty takes hold, and the people are in no better condition than they were before the discovery.

Reliance on a natural resource, export driven model can also create a problem with financial responsibility by those in command. To retain power, politicians may have reduced taxes to zero, relied on income from state controlled extraction and export of natural resources, and misappropriated funds for their own political agendas. The population has little or no incentive to keep those in power financially accountable since they do not pay taxes anyway, and those who created the problems continue perpetuating a system of poor decisions. The lion's share of the income from exportation does not find its way to social services, infrastructure development, or the population in general. The abundance of natural resources can even give rise to corruption and poor governance.

Poor governance is the third development trap identified by Paul Collier. Sometimes a nation's leadership makes long-term, sustainable decisions when they are in a position of great potential and wealth. The nation of Dubai, for example, invested heavily in infrastructure and tourism development when it was still rich in oil reserves. Many nations do not consider long-term implications of the pillage, plunder and export model, however. This leaves the wealth of a nation in the bank accounts of other countries, people, or corporations, and an otherwise middle-income, emerging nation becomes or remains in abject poverty. Further problems are realized when governments adopt protectionist trade policies, implement burdensome tax policies, or create conditions of uncertainty[18]. Zimbabwe is the poster-country for poor governance, uncertainty, and bad policy, and will be discussed later. Robert Mugabe is a leader who moved an entire nation from a position of strength and growth to a poor, stagnant environment with a dismal outlook.

Sometimes nations are simply unlucky. Countries may escape conflict, be rich in resources, and have excellent government policies, but they are cursed by geography. A nation that is

---

[18] Uncertainty is among the best ways to destroy an economy, even the United States economy was slowed through 2013 from the uncertainty created by the indecision and gridlock produced in Congress.

completely landlocked may lack the benefits from access to world markets ocean access provides. They may have distrustful, disruptive, or aggressive neighbors, and may not be able to negotiate proper access to roads or rivers to attain access to the ocean and world markets. Without access to markets for exportation, nations cannot import consumer goods or export raw materials. Adam Smith wrote, *"As by means of water-carriage a more extensive market is opened to every sort of industry than what land-carriage alone can afford it, so it is upon the sea-coast, and along the banks of navigable rivers, that industry of every kind naturally begins to subdivide and improve itself, and it is frequently not till a long time after that those improvements extend themselves to the inland parts of the country."*

The geography curse is not just that of a nation being land-locked; though being land-locked can play a large role, climate and topography play important roles as well. People in nations with large mountainous regions may find it difficult to farm or transport their goods to world markets. Travelling becomes difficult in mountainous terrain, and transaction costs for conducting trade will increase. Their expense and their products can become non-competitive on the world market when they are left with no choice except to increase their prices to account for the increased cost of production and delivery.

Various climates can promote diseases like malaria and harm public health, which affects output, overall. Drought can affect farm output, just as monsoons can. Reliance on regular weather events can press societies already living on the margin into starvation or worse when weather patterns are different than expected. Dry climates can become too wet, wet climates can become too dry, cold regions can be too hot, hot regions can be too cold, and traditional farm output that relies on farmers' expectations on meteorological consistency can be directly affected.

Wealthy nations' people enjoy insurance on their crops in the event of a drought or flood event. They can treat health conditions as they arise, and benefit from access to world markets and imports during bad years and exports during good years. The developing world does not have insurance or modern healthcare, and often does not have access to world markets. With reliance on predictive models, stable governments, peaceful environments, and access to good infrastructure and world markets, the people of poor nations are always at risk from unexpected income, weather, political, or economic shocks. Living on the margin, as those in abject poverty do, means that any change can be catastrophic, slow already anemic growth, and further constrain those already chained to the bottom of the economic ladder.

These are only four of the many, many problems faced by developing nations. They have their place, and all are equally valid points to the problems that face the developing world. The list does not end with only conflict, resources, governance, or geography, however. Each of these problems has many caveats and subcategories. The problem of world poverty is complicated and far reaching. To solve it we must recognize how deep it truly goes and what it will take to address such interlaced and pervasive problems.

Chapter 7: Solving World Poverty: Unorthodox Approach

"The difference between a kleptocrat and a wise statesman, between a robber baron and a public benefactor, is merely one of degree."

– Jared Diamond

Redefining the Problem

Bottom billion nations no longer have the ability to bring themselves from their perpetual state of abject poverty. Among the problems that have been defined so far are a lack of private property rights, education, infrastructure, healthcare, geography, natural resources, poor governance and institutions, warfare, access to proper banking, and a past intertwined in all the problems associated with colonialism. Other authors have identified an even longer, more diffuse list of things that contribute to world poverty:

> No natural resources, too many natural resources, climate, topography, political relations with neighboring nations, internal ethnic and political divisions, proximity to world markets, poor trade policies, poor monetary policy, convertibility of currency, poor industrial policy, too much foreign debt, not enough foreign aid, excessive government intervention in markets, excessive government spending, too much state ownership, military or revolutionary conflict, poor institutions, lack of banking access, access to investors, lack of capital, brain drain, and aid that has gone wrong or been executed poorly.

All these problems can be traced to a much more elemental problem. The free market cannot emerge to repair these broken societies because they lack at least some of the four basic economic factors of production: Land (natural resources are often abundant but impossible to develop without the other three factors, and property rights are often trampled out by the government), Labor (the people are often sick and unable to work or have no other choice except to stay home and protect their property and children), Capital (human knowledge and training, infrastructure, and physical equipment), and Entrepreneurship (investors, inventors, and innovators). Foreign aid to developing nations is necessary if we hope to eliminate poverty on earth, especially if the goal is to eradicate poverty by 2030 as stated by the *Millennium Development Goals* developed by the United Nations.

It's already been discussed how communities may substitute in favor of free food over local entrepreneurs. This substitution is not simply a shock to the local economy that can be seen as a freak occurrence. Impoverished communities receive perennial aid in many settings, and over time people forget their craft. Skills are forgotten or never passed from father to son or mother to daughter. The factors of production, learned by every first semester under-graduate economics student, can be lost or mitigated. Impoverished economies lack the quantity of land, labor, capital, and entrepreneurship that will be prerequisite for continued growth and development out of unceasing poverty.

Historically, capable families of entrepreneurs no longer want to build businesses. One of the findings that Duflo and Banerjee introduce in their book, *"Poor Economics,"* is that many families hope their children will grow up to acquire stable jobs in government or industry. They are not seeking to innovate; they simply want some form of stability, and they do not value entrepreneurship in the same way it is valued in developed countries. Decreased valuation on entrepreneurship creates a drain on the economy, innovation is stifled, and otherwise productive people adopt rent-seeking behaviors over industrious output. Even with an emphasis on other ways to earn a living, there are no shortages of entrepreneurs in the developing world; often black markets are thriving. Unfortunately their activities are hampered by over-zealous politicians, unenforced or unwritten laws, or the absence of access to proper courts to decide disputes. In addition, they are often lacking access to banks, investors, and larger markets even when their rights are protected by clear legal definitions, laws, and courts.

Furthermore, there is a shortage of industry to acquire a normal, 40-hour per week job. This creates an environment where the existing entrepreneurs are competing with so many others in the exact same business that their profitability is severely degraded. Duflo and Banerjee discuss this problem in detail. To sum it up briefly, entrepreneurs who operate a shop with a little inventory may see very few customers in a day, thus very little profit is earned. Even adding variety or increasing inventory does little to improve the state of their business because there are often many others selling the same products and no access to larger markets to justify scaling up their operation. The business owners do not earn enough to justify expansion, nor do they have available options to change careers. They remain in business, impoverished, and indebted while living day to day without the possibility of saving just a little to get ahead.

Entrepreneurship is also hindered by a lack of human capital, which is also in short supply. Often entrepreneurs do not know how to scale up their businesses even when their business activity might be thriving by local standards. They may not understand that their high margin goods on the small scale could be exploited to make larger profits on a larger scale [52]. For example, assume one of our poor entrepreneurs is selling food at a price of $0.50 that costs her $0.25 per unit to make. This is an accounting profit of 50%! Our vendor may decide not to scale up because doing so would mean much of her supply might spoil when it goes unsold. What she fails to understand is that selling 10 units per day might earn her $5.00 per day, $2.50 net profit without spoilage, but making 100 units where possibly 25 go unsold and spoil will yield a far greater $37.50 in sales and a net profit of $12.50. This larger amount would allow for better equipment, possibly an employee or two, and more. Certainly this $10.00 difference would yield an incredible improvement to her standard of living.

This problem is not unique to poor countries, although it is more pronounced. Even in places like the United States, people often start businesses without the proper understanding of how to do their accounting, complete profit and loss calculations, or acquire bank loans to boost them through slumps in sales. My father has been a business consultant for many years. One story he consistently tells about new clients relates to their poor accounting practices and horrible management. Clients who are American born, American educated, and retain an abundance of human capital paid for by American taxpayers are often still led down the shameful hall to bankruptcy. If they had applied for a simple consolidation loan they may have successfully turned their business completely around.

My father tells another story as well. Clients sometimes think they are broke simply because they do not account for incomes and payments properly. He often finds over-payments to the IRS and money owed from customers, all of which would have been discovered if they had marked transactions in their ledger correctly. The money owed to his clients is sometimes in the hundreds of thousands of dollars, and these are small business owners in the United States! Imagine how much worse it must be for those who do not benefit from the 12 years of education, functioning markets, and experiences freely provided in our rich society.

For small businesses who do not understand the very basics of banking, accounting, and management their future is uncertain at best and dire otherwise. Millions of dollars are wasted and lives are ruined. Employees, owners, and families all feel the pain of these business failures, but at least they have the option to find a job in another similar business, a new industry, or even the opportunity to start another business. Extrapolate this same mismanagement problem to the developing world, where there are few jobs to substitute for failed enterprises, few banks from which to borrow funds to start a larger business or grow an existing one, and also a shortage of human capital. One can easily see that these problems are surely worse under the long shadow of extreme poverty.

Even farming is affected by a lack of human capital. Not understanding how to correctly use fertilizer, for example, may result in improper fertilization [52]. Over-fertilizing the ground can have as equal an impact as under-fertilizing since both harm agricultural yields. Over use of fertilizer can even damage the watershed, create dead zones, and possibly kill the fish – which could be otherwise utilized for protein – in nearby rivers or lakes. Over-fertilizing means increased costs with little or no benefit, and under-fertilizing means decreased yields and lower margins. Farmers do not always understand proper fertilization quantities and techniques and simply choose not to fertilize their crops at all, or even if they do understand the methods they may lack the funds to buy the fertilizer.

Commercial banking is often absent or inadequate, and private property rights are not always formalized for the conversion of land into a collateralized debt, so loans can also be difficult to acquire. Under these conditions convincing a bank to issue a loan can be nearly impossible, especially if farmers cannot properly and confidently present their expectation for higher yields. They may not even believe the higher yields are possible, simply because they do not have the proper knowledge, experience, or education requisite for such a belief.

Farmers also frequently lack the knowledge necessary to exploit the benefits of highly productive forms of high-yield seeds, which are also more expensive [52]. They may choose not to purchase high-yield seeds, since they may lack funds and access to bank loans, and because they do not have a proper understanding of their benefits to justify such an investment. They might be afraid of experiencing some form of an environmental shock that directly affects the season's harvest. Without insurance against crop failure, they might find investment into better seeds too risky.

Farmers' risk aversion may actually make them poorer; ironically, their saving to insure against crop failure and decreased income also ensures a lower yield and decreased potential income. Farmers in the developing world are afraid a bad crop will mean their entire investment is lost; thus, they choose the cheaper, short-term option of normal seeds and no fertilizer. With better understanding and knowledge, they could save to self-insure against a bad yield, utilize the correct amounts of fertilizer, acquire funds from banks (when banks are nearby and property can be converted into collateral), buy better seeds, and achieve better crop yields on average. Unfortunately, without experience or education they simply do not understand the results of the cost-benefit analysis.

Some farmers have been farming for decades, passing knowledge on to their children and grandchildren, and do have the experience to see the benefits of high yield seeds and fertilizer. They understand the benefits of capital equipment and know how to use it to harvest more from their lands. Unfortunately, developing nations are sometimes led down the road from breadbasket to basket-case where private property rights are abused, degraded, or destroyed when corrupt leadership redistributes assets. No amount of human or physical capital can save a farmer from bad governance. Bad governance that results in the redistribution of assets can destroy faith in the economy and make investment very risky, capital difficult to acquire, and loanable funds impossible to find. Furthermore, it can leave experienced farmers fleeing the nation and novice farmers with large swaths of land they have no idea how to efficiently farm, or equipment they have no idea how to use.

Another problem can occur where aid has been rampant in a nation for many decades. The human capital that would have been passed from generation to generation (to generation) can be lost. When aid comes in the form of donations, markets can be destroyed and existing entrepreneurs may lose their ability to sell their products while facing competition from free goods. When this type of aid occurs over decades, generations of people lose their need to acquire traditional skills, and human capital is degraded. After a few generations, a time frame of 20-40 years, the loss of human capital manifests in idle populations or inefficient production. This is more clear when considering, like the previous paragraph, the farmer and his descendants. This loss of human capital can occur even more quickly when families are atrophied due to fatal illness such as tuberculosis, malaria, or HIV/AIDS. When discussing HIV/AIDS and the effect on a family from the death of a mother and father, Jeffrey Sachs writes, *"The oldest child takes charge, but has not yet had time to master proper farming techniques. The next crop fails, and the children must depend on other households in the village. The family income has declined to zero because the level of technological knowledge has actually declined"* [2]. Since about 70% of all the people in the world who live with HIV/AIDS live in Africa [68], and more are affected by other diseases, a village is often hit by this sequence of events for more than just one family and entire communities are negatively impacted.

Even when it is not a loss of human capital, it could have been a loss of land-tenure. Without proper mechanisms in place to leave land to one's children and grandchildren, experience passed from one generation to the next might be lost when it becomes unusable. This is more frequent in basket-case economies where the government redistributes inheritances arbitrarily, instead of allowing producers to take over where their parents and grandparents left off. Natural resource production and farm yields alike are harmed since experience is lost and capital accumulation is made more difficult. The economy remains stagnant or shrinks under this type of political pressure; the standard of living falls, and entire populations suffer.

Self-discipline is another human-capital related problem faced by the poor. This problem is not unique to the developing world; in fact, it is seen in the industrialized world as well and often manifests to some extent in rural communities. This is not to say people in these communities, poor or rural, are unable to self-govern their activities or that they are lazy; they are often very hard working. The type of self-discipline I am referring to has to do with how people save and invest for the future. When they are not compelled to save or they have improper options for saving, people often encounter incidental costs, like medical expenses, and they spend their funds. When families do not have funds available, they may choose another form of treatment or wait to see if their health improves on its own, but the availability of savings changes their decision tree.

Given options for saving that are not as easy to withdraw for those incidental expenses, poor people may be able to lock away some money for rough times. The goal would be for them to find a way to solve their problems in the same way they would if they had no savings available. Some farmers, for example, may buy their fertilizer as soon as they harvest their crop and sell it. They can store the fertilizer until the next planting season, and it is not easily converted into cash, so the funds are not wasted on incidental expenses in the interim. Proper banking can also create this mechanism. Banerjee and Duflo present, however, that impoverished families may hold back some from saving since they fear an incidental expense may occur and they will not have access to their money. Saving rates remain low and capital investment does not improve [52].

Without proper savings or access to banks, it can be very difficult to find affordable, loanable funds to acquire capital. The poor are often led to borrow from what we in the West would define as loan-sharks – people who may loan capital or money at a high interest rate and make it very difficult for people to get out of debt. The poor may borrow on a small scale, but after their earnings for the day they end up owing most of what they earned back to the loan-shark. The loss of profit to interest payments puts them in a perpetual cycle of daily borrowing and a hand to mouth existence. No matter how hard they work, they find it very difficult to save or earn enough to invest in the future without still borrowing from the local loan-shark. Discouraged, their productivity can be harmed and their perpetual state of poverty can be worsened.

Even with access to loanable funds, the poor can rarely acquire the amount necessary to purchase the proper levels of physical capital to scale their production. Micro-lending has done quite a lot for pushing small businesses into the realm of expansion and global scaling, but it does not do much for the farmer in need of a tractor. Lacking the private property rights to their land, it is often impossible to convert farmland into collateral for a loan to the scale necessary to purchase larger or more expensive farm equipment.

Some countries, like Zimbabwe, have even gone as far as to disastrously break up large farms into smaller, family-sized plots and redistribute the land from the wealthy to the poor. This practice collapsed private property rights and destroyed the possibility for loanable funds to be distributed where they might be most needed and best utilized. Zimbabwe was Africa's breadbasket prior to 1999, producing much of the continent's cereals and grains. Though it only grew at a rate of about 1.18% per year during the preceding fifteen years, it was nowhere near as poor as it became following the 1999 election. The communist leadership had exhausted its usefulness, was corrupted, and the nation was experiencing increasing inflation and unemployment levels. Instead of allowing new leadership and market based reform, Robert Mugabe (the president at the time) consolidated power and undertook land reforms that effectively decimated their economy. From 1998-2008

Zimbabwe shrank at an average rate of 6.09% per year while its neighbors' growth ranged from 4-5% per year. By 2012 the economy was 36% smaller than it had been in 1999. Foreign direct investment shrank from a maximum of $444 million per year to a lackluster $3.8 million by 2003. Ranking 176th (the U.S. ranks 12th by comparison) on The Heritage Foundation's 2014 Index of Economic Freedom, it still has not returned to its previous levels of foreign direct investment [69].

More problems occur for those in need where capital is not functional and the population does not have the proper knowledge (another human capital problem) to repair or rebuild equipment, or to operate the commercial machinery – like in Zimbabwe after the industrial farms were expropriated from their owners in 1999. Lacking the human capital necessary to conduct commercial farming, many resort to subsistence farming practices. They may rely on aid workers to do repairs to equipment or simply let the equipment sit idle, like when Robert Mugabe ordered farm production to cease [70]. Even if they did know how to complete repairs themselves, it may be time consuming to acquire the necessary replacement parts. Since the farm expropriation violated the tenure of private property holders, and because of the subsistence farm output, many industrial producers have simply closed their operations and replacement parts are only available through importation. Without the competence to repair the equipment and without fast access to replacement parts from abroad, capital investment may seem like bad investment to already weary entrepreneurs.

In economies where human capital is in such short supply, the poor often miscalculate the benefit of even a few years of education. Just investing a few years in early education can result in great increases in income later in life, and possibly problem solving ability as young people grow older [52]. Since the world's poor populations fail to invest in human capital for young people, or try picking one child to educate over the rest, human capital is greatly ignored. With such misunderstanding of the benefits of education, it is not surprising that the adults often still do not understand the needs for education and continue not to conduct proper cost-benefit analysis. When it comes to investment versus consumption, impoverished people often choose consumption "today" over the investment of capital to improve production and realize increased consumption "tomorrow." The future is uncertain, more for the developing world than for the post-industrialized world, and poor populations choose subsistence today over possible starvation tomorrow – ironically to their dismay.

Another form of physical capital is also frequently missing in the developing world: infrastructure. The government often fails to invest in adequate levels of infrastructure such as roads, railways, highways, sanitation, clean water, electrical grids, ports, etc., and does not invest to enhance or improve economic activity. In nations without such infrastructure, transport of goods overland or through rivers is made more difficult and the cost of trade is increased. Furthermore, developing nations' governments may not invest the money, time and effort necessary to create agreements for cross border infrastructure, nor the will or funds to build such projects. Without cross border investment, nations that need access to world markets are left without said access.

Even when countries have access to foreign markets they may be inhibited by their lack of infrastructure and funds to develop it. The problem is circular, unfortunately, since trade would be easier and national income and tax revenues would increase with improved infrastructure, but trade is unattractive in nations that lack infrastructure and do not have the funds to build it. Funds that would be available if they had access to international markets and could be used to build infrastructure may not manifest in these nations; therefore, they are disconnected from international markets and unable to conduct much needed trade. Unimproved infrastructure results in less income, and less income results in fewer tax revenues for the government; existing infrastructure deteriorates.

Labor is also hindered by the outbreak or limited treatment of diseases like malaria, cholera, various worms, diarrhea, AIDS, tuberculosis, and many other ailments. Illnesses increase absenteeism and decrease morale. Productivity is degraded and business output declines. Some illnesses, such as AIDS, create emotional and work related stress as people are concerned for health instead of occupation. Life expectancies are limited by illnesses and long-term skill sets are lost to death or debilitation. Increased medical costs reduce saving, demand, and investment in an economy.

Improper investment into disease reducing infrastructure, like sanitation, also contributes to continued poverty. According to *Water.org*, every 21 seconds a child dies from a water-related illness. The World Health Organization reports that in 2010 women spent 200 million hours each day collecting water that is often dirty or contaminated [71]. Almost a billion people live on earth without proper levels of clean water and sanitation, and that contributes to even greater poverty. Without proper sanitation human waste contributes to disease, and without clean water, waterborne illnesses create sickness and reduce productivity. With such an impact on labor, we see how important public health can be to a people and an economy.

Lacking entrepreneurs who are willing to take on these risks limits the way businesses grow and operate. It limits the motivations of populations and changes their motivations. They dream of stability instead of great reward that often accompanies risk. This reduces innovation and stifles otherwise enterprising minds. A shortage of capital, both human and physical, has hampered the productivity of the developing world. The need for private property rights and natural resources, such as the simple necessity of clean water, has created an environment of uncertainty and eliminated the convertibility of assets into collateral. Labor has been affected by the lack of sanitation and clean water, and millions of hours are wasted every day collecting resources instead of productive activity. It has even been estimated that the collection of drinking water costs the whole of Africa nearly 40 billion hours (the entire level of a year's output in France) per year [72]. The factors of production are vital to the success and development of every country, but only in the developing world are all four missing in some significant capacity and contributing to their continual economic hardship.

One Billion Drops

There are over one billion people in the developing world who have an immense amount of untapped potential. They could be employed, cheaply, to produce many of the goods that are consumed all around the world. The standard of living could be improved for everyone if we could only tap the immense lake of potential from these people. If somehow we could improve their health, secure their property rights, educate them, and provide them the capital to produce, then everyone could benefit. The developing nations' populations would find gainful employment, even at a low wage, while the consumers of the world could enjoy less expensive consumer goods. Like a billion drops of water, the people in our world are lakes of potential just waiting to be productive if they just had an estuary in which to start flowing. Outside investors are the estuary, with an ability to organize labor within impoverished nations and to connecting it with world markets. With a safe harbor and protection from theft or government expropriation, foreign direct investment will improve and the great potential of the lake can finally be released.

Allowing the labor to flow is not enough, however. Labor alone will only produce subsistence-level results, which will only accomplish continued poverty, though perhaps with some hope for natural improvement in the future. To better realize the potential of such a vast resource, one billion laborers, the developing world also needs capital. Like a dam produces useful energy from a lake as the water flows down the river, so too can capital produce useful output as labor is made more productive through the use of better tools, equipment, and facilities. Further improvements can be realized through cleaner work environments, health facilities, and education. The lake of potential can be converted into an ocean of productivity if there is investment into human and physical capital.

Arable land and other natural resources are not in short supply in the developing world. Oil, diamonds, gold, rare earth metals, even water are all resources that can be utilized for the conversion from developing to emerging economies. Investment is risky where private property rights are capricious, though, so we cannot carry people from poverty without first formalizing those rights. Capital is not convertible into productive capacity if the natural resources cannot be utilized as collateral for loanable funds. Land can directly transform an economy from impossibly impoverished to potentially enriched through the formalization process of private property.

Creating a fungible system of property rights is difficult, and simply assigning ownership is not sufficient for its creation. In the words of Hernando DeSoto, *"They must identify and gather up the existing property representations scattered throughout their nations and bring them into one integrated system to give the assets of all their citizens the fungibility, bureaucratic machinery, and network required to produce capital."* [65] What DeSoto means is that the informal arrangements often accepted and utilized for local transactions need to be formalized on a national scale, defined at the county level, and protected at the local level. With the advent of computers and the subsequent reduction in record keeping costs, this has never been more possible to accomplish.

DeSoto also writes, *"The problem with extralegal social contracts is that their property representations are not sufficiently codified and fungible to have a broad range of application outside their own geographical parameters."* [65] Once ownership is defined, easily transferable, and protected from illegal expropriation, local populations can convert the property into a representation of intangible, abstract value. Any previously existing arrangements that were made outside the law will have been formalized and property will be convertible to real value, making it bankable and realizing the possibility for capital acquisition.

Intangible abstract value is necessary for the conversion of assets, like land, into capital. Once banks can make loans that are collateralized by the newly formalized property, land owners can use the loans to acquire the quantity of capital needed for improved levels of production. Employment levels will rise, output will improve, and the timer on poverty's eradication will finally begin to tick. Once property rights are no longer unpredictable, banks too will have an incentive to invest in developing areas of the world and no excuse to avoid those most in need.

Some of the issues the poorest people in the world face have been identified and presented in a way that makes it seem like poverty is an easy problem to solve. Unfortunately, the investment into any one of these categories will only illuminate the shortcomings of the other categories, and poverty is an extremely complex issue. To see real growth and have real potential to defeat world poverty, the world will have to invest in all the factors of production simultaneously. If the underlying problems relate to land, labor, capital, and entrepreneurship, then surely they can be easily tracked to the already defined surface problems – namely private property rights, health, poor infrastructure, and bad governance.

Defining private property rights is important, but not sufficient for development in a nation where the population is dying from AIDS or malaria. Curing disease and making labor productive is necessary, but not sufficient in a nation with a poor or crumbling infrastructure that inhibits access to outside markets. A state of the art infrastructure is a great way to provide access to outside markets, but it is not sufficient when prohibitive public policies hinder business and entrepreneurial activity. Even the least corrupt and well-meaning government, one that acts on behalf of the people and hopes to develop into the 21st century with a healthy population and friendly relations with its neighbors, cannot raise the revenues necessary to pay for public investments if outside investors fear an environment where private property rights are endangered or simply do not exist. With such a vicious circle for development, it is clear that there is no single area where an entity could focus its efforts with any measureable and sustainable expectation for success. All the factors of production must be repaired simultaneously.

Non-governmental organizations (NGOs) mostly have their own specialization and can often do great work where they are employed. However, none have the funds available to attack every shortcoming any particular nation may have. Most do not even have the funds or skills necessary to attack every shortcoming of any individual community. William Easterly cheekily comments, *"Aid agencies are like Yosemite Sam, firing at random in all directions."* [58] He is right, as funny as the statement might seem. Economists have known since Adam Smith wrote in 1776 that specializing is the most effective way to achieve one's production goals. Aid agencies are no different, and though many do specialize, far too many attempt to attack many poverty perpetuating problems at once. It's like the "honey-do list" my wife gives me. I need to trim my shrubs, mow my lawn, repair the toilet, replace all the power outlets, and more. I could easily accomplish any one of these tasks and move to the next one. If I take the top off the toilet, the screws out of the outlet, place the sheers by the shrubs, gas up my lawnmower, drain the water from my toilet, pull the cover off only one outlet, make one cut on the shrubs, and push the mower into the lawn, then all I've managed to do is upset my wife since I did not finish anything. Consider all the time it took me simply to move from each task to the next without ever focusing or completing any particular one.

I've just stated that every problem needs to be attacked at once, but that each agency should specialize in their respective field.

To attack every problem at once while specializing on only one problem at a time is somewhat contradictory, but that is also why I've written every section of this book with a theme of finding solutions under the given set of circumstances. In the 21st century there is one organization that has the resources, access to the political powerbases of every nation, the rolodex to all the world's most influential experts, and the ability to organize the activities of many separate entities. The United Nations can take charge and direct the activities of every NGO in the world. The U.N. does not need to take over any agencies, or mandate any activities by any agencies, only to provide guidance. By redirecting efforts and promoting specialization among the NGOs, the expertise of the various agencies can be fully utilized. The U.N. can stack the efforts of many NGOs to fill every need at once in communities as each of the missing factors of production are identified. We can finally end poverty, ironically through a centrally-planned model of development. The U.N. has already taken a large step to that end with the Millennium Development Goals, Millennium Development Villages, and the Universal Declaration of Human Rights, but they can go even further, and with greater success. The argument for the above suggested action is strengthened in the following sections and a call to action is presented to finalize this chapter.

The state of our world is well-known, every economist and most world leaders understand the poverty problem, and there are literally thousands of non-governmental organizations with millions of employees and volunteers who are working to alleviate the suffering every day. Organizing and directing the NGOs has not been attempted on a world-wide scale so far. The reason is clear: most people, governments, and especially the United Nations find it somewhat intrusive for a central organization to direct the efforts of privately operating firms.

However, it may be necessary if we realistically expect to conquer poverty. Billions of dollars flow from all over the world, into weak or diffuse interventions, and much moves through government hands. Large amounts of money flow into NGO efforts as well but only marginal improvements are realized. Like a natural disaster, undirected efforts lead to inefficient results with longer recovery times.

Napoleon's Approach

Early in the 20th century the world was faced with new knowledge of development and awoke to the impoverished state of the developing world. The West knew it had ravaged many fruitful regions of the world, and following the panics of 1893 and 1907, while also facing the prospect of world war, many people were searching for a better system of government and economic management. Marx had published his ideas decades before and the conditions of the time seemed perfect for their real-world implementation and experimentation. Throughout the 20th century, nations experimented with fascism, socialism, communism, and capitalism. It seems capitalism is the best of the flawed systems that have been created to date, but it is far from perfect. Many market economies are still adopting socialist policies and moving toward a more mixed system, and it is possible we will find an ideal compromise of "Social-Capitalism" at some point in the future.

The developed world can make choices and debate whether more socialist or capitalist leaning policies are more effective and better for their peoples or nations' growth rates, but the developing world does not have that luxury. Free market ideals will take over and drive the population into prosperity in the presence of good governance or a benevolent leadership, so the argument goes. The invisible hand will direct entrepreneurs to create business activity, increase their own standard of living, and, by default, employ those who would otherwise be unemployed. Products desirable for production will come to market and undesirable items will disappear. Titans of industry will emerge, resources will be automatically directed to their most efficient use, and markets will self-organize into a perpetual economic development machine; however, this perpetual economic development machine does not always come to pass. In reality, sometimes markets simply fail, no titans emerge, and no entrepreneurs rise to innovate. Resources are often used inefficiently, abused to the point of non-existence, or abandoned entirely.

In the absence of market-driven economies it stands to reason that a centralized authority should take over – at least in the short term. The questions are when is the right time and what sort of centralized governance would be best? The great military commander, Napoleon Bonaparte, was known to have spoken many times about how he was able to adapt his army to the circumstances. William Duggan wrote on this topic, *"Napoleon stress[ed] how he never tried to impose his will on circumstances. Rather, he yielded to them"* [73]. Yielding to circumstances is precisely the argument; the state of the world and the level of technology dictates how we should attempt to eradicate world poverty. Markets and central planning have both failed to help bring developing nations past the bottom rung of the economic ladder. NGOs have helped developing nations somewhat, but ultimately they too have failed to help them escape poverty. The U.N. has thus far also failed and continues to flounder. The IMF and World Bank spend billions of dollars in loans and loan forgiveness, ultimately to no avail. The West has been imposing its will and its plans on the developing world for decades, but has not been successful. We have ignored the wisdom of Napoleon, instead of searching the developing world for local answers to their blight. Worse, we have diluted our efforts almost to the point of futility, when consolidation of resources and tailoring interventions to the needs of various communities would easily have achieved many development objectives.

Poverty is a Natural Disaster

After living through the tornado that ravaged Joplin, MO, it was clear to me that sometimes central authority is necessary. When the storm had finished destroying one third of the city, disaster management officials arrived to organize labor, direct search and rescue, and plan cleanup and rebuilding efforts through their centralized direction. City and emergency management leadership set up a command center at a fire station nearby and directed the efforts of every sub-organization involved. Charity organizations were asked to set up their operations in at least three strategic locations around the city. They were then tasked with their specialty, distribution of much needed food, water, clothing, and shelter. Americorps was employed to recruit volunteers and bus them to locations where emergency personnel were waiting to direct their search and rescue efforts. Police were tasked with blocking entry into various parts of the city, protecting civilians from unstable piles of rubble, guarding undamaged areas from looting, and keeping search and rescue personnel safe from molestation. Doctors and nurses were sent to several locations all over the ravaged area to treat simple wounds, give tetanus shots, and conduct triage. Mental health workers were directed in other ways to assist. Through radios, maps, telephones, and advisors from FEMA, fire, police and even military, reports came in from various forward operational bases, plans were adapted, and new orders were issued. The efforts were seamless, many scared people were rescued, and the death toll, though high, was minimized.

Information was centralized and disseminated periodically, and efforts were rarely, if ever, duplicated. It is possible leadership would have surfaced in time without the centralized authority that arrived and took control, but it probably would have been in random pockets in smaller portions of communities, with fewer resources, less equipment, and no knowledge of their own need in other parts of the city. Volunteers may not have arrived from outside the city or state, and even if they had come they may have found it difficult to find where they could become most useful. After a time there may still have been a single leader or central committee that emerged to make decisions on behalf of the population, but it could easily have taken weeks that those buried in rubble did not have. Assuming leadership emerged quickly, activities would still have been centrally planned by that leadership in the short term – months or years, after the storm. The short term for an economic disaster is on the order of decades, however, not months or years.

Much like what happens after a natural disaster, a centralized authority to direct the use of labor and resources is necessary. Since failed economies are a disaster – even referred to as basket-case economies in some instances – they should be treated in the same way. They sometimes need a centrally-planned jump start. Just like disaster areas need disaster management authorities to direct activities, failed economies need an economic management authority to direct development once they fall beyond the point of a natural correction.

Unfortunately, ideologically entrenched arguments often take sway over more reasonable, germane logic, and so far no central leadership has emerged to effectively manage the cleanup. Institutions like The World Bank, International Monetary Fund, World Health Organization, and United Nations have done a lot, and continue to do a lot, but development still remains too diffuse. Over 40,000 NGOs exist in the world, undirected, and not reporting to any specific central authority. In effect, a splattering of effort is taking place all across the globe, which any painter can report is a very ineffective way of covering a wall with a quality coat of paint. Yosemite Sam is alive and well and just as inaccurate as ever.

A Feasible Plan to Eradicate Poverty

Like a large corporation that must manage many regions, districts, and branches, solving world poverty should be managed like a business and treated like a disaster. The United Nations acts in a political capacity but has no true constituency; therefore, it is unique in that it can also organize efforts in a corporate fashion without regard to reelection or taxpayer money. The U.N. must manage its own budget, to be sure, but by centralizing development efforts the flow of that money can become more transparent and more effective at the same time. The cost to the U.N. for attacking development like a natural disaster could be minimized by utilizing NGOs over or in addition to U.N. agencies. Already existing agencies of the UN, like UNICEF and the UNDP (United Nations Development Programme), can be used for more technical interventions when NGOs fall short of expertise or government contacts. The United Nations can manage all development efforts and centrally direct the efforts of NGOs, while also advising governments on how best to overcome their greatest shortcomings.

To some extent the U.N. already operates to advise many governments on development and NGOs can register with the U.N. for direction. However, the effort needed to find information on where NGOs should be operating for maximum effect is somewhat difficult to locate for the normal, enterprising philanthropist. Perhaps the U.N. should operate more like a corporation, directing the efforts of NGOs based on information it gets from field agents, other NGOs, and regional directors already working on the ground in various development areas.

The UNDP budget for 2014 is about $1.555 Billion, and they have over 700 ongoing projects to alleviate poverty around the world [74]. With more information readily available at a centralized office, and a plan to direct their efforts, NGOs could be better utilized to fight poverty all over the world. To some extent the Millennium Villages prove this point. With an investment of about $300,000 per village per year for five years, the U.N. has directed efforts to provide high-yield seeds, fertilizers, medicines, drinking wells, schools, clinics, insecticide-treated bed nets, antiretroviral drugs, Internet access, and more. Fourteen sites across ten different countries are benefiting from U.N. efforts to combat poverty and are well on their way to self-sufficiency. The Millennium Village project is new in that it is a laser-focused approach that fills every void at once in the villages where it operates, and is superior to the traditional scattershot approach (my honey-do list) that accomplished only a few goals in thousands of places all over the globe. The U.N. is directly managing and funding these efforts with the help of only a few NGO groups.

With the more than 5000 U.N. registered NGOs, and the 40,000 NGOs that exist worldwide, the U.N. could easily direct efforts to complete many more village projects similar to the

Millennium Villages on a greatly expanded basis, and not even at their own expense. Since NGOs usually specialize in only a few types of intervention, U.N. direction of NGO efforts could place several organizations to work in the same locations from an office at the U.N. headquarters in New York, and via a website that lists every organization, where it is operating, and what it is doing.

The U.N. could make the process of development operations simple by listing what is needed and where. NGOs could be directed to operate in specific communities in conjunction with other NGOs, and still operate to fulfill their own objectives through their own specialization. With consolidated effort the NGOs could work in harmony to attack every shortcoming from each of the four factors of production simultaneously, wherever they observe a need or receive a request. If something is missing the local U.N. assigned officers (who could easily be assigned from the NGOs themselves at $0.00 cost to the UN) could report back to the regional command who could inform the central office at the UN. As needs are highlighted resources could be redirected from the central U.N. office. Poverty can be eradicated.

Like a corporation depends on regional directors to communicate with district level managers that direct the efforts of store level employees, so too could the U.N. adopt this type of management structure. They could create country level U.N. offices (some already exist in several nations) that report to regional U.N. officers. Regional officers would communicate directly with U.N. headquarters in New York City. Once field officers identify what local areas need, they could inform their regional officer and NGOs could then be assigned the task of filling that need. NGOs could act as field officers, learning needs and informing the regional U.N. officers, and development goals could be clearly identified for everyone to see via the website. When a group of NGOs decides to attack all the problems in a particular village, or learns more needs exist in a location where it is already operating, that information could be identified on the website and at headquarters as well. In this way we could avoid duplicating efforts, undertaking unsustainable or futile efforts, or damaging local economies. Furthermore, the U.N. could highlight safety issues and assist with keeping NGO workers safe during their selfless efforts.

The IMF and World Bank could also be freed to accomplish their 21st century mandates. The IMF could focus more on short-term lending to governments, and help volatile regions of the world attain more stability. More stability would yield better economic outcomes, and they might even expand their efforts into subverting corruption. The World Bank could continue making development loans to governments who wish to build infrastructure. It could focus efforts to gain the most benefit from spending by observing where the U.N. was directing NGOs and then plan accordingly. Every development agency could be better utilized for proper development and the flailing system, as it exists today, could become a well-oiled development machine.

The one item NGOs would likely have trouble with is creating the private property rights necessary for any economic improvement. The U.N. would need to utilize their contacts at the national level in countries where they are already operating, to modernize the process for creating private property rights. Information on the informal recognition of property rights, from the ground level NGO efforts, could be used for the creation of formalized national property rights, customized to existing local arrangements, and sensitive to local cultures.

The U.N. could also assist nations in streamlining the creation of a legal framework for resolving disputes as formalized deeds are created. By assigning teams of advisers, U.N. or otherwise, people's rights to their land could be safeguarded throughout the process and national sovereignty could be protected. Without proper systems and mechanisms in place to support the efforts placed to develop the factors of production, all our other efforts are meaningless. Private property rights, and a clear, simple system for the acquisition of said property rights, are absolutely paramount to the development of national economies. Private property rights must originate at the local level but be enforced from the federal level downward. Unfortunately, corruption is sure to rear its ugly head in this process as productive properties are surely going to tempt the less than ethical government officials or crime bosses. Since corruption is a clear problem in many locations around the world, the U.N. must also direct efforts toward it as well.

Subvert Corruption

A playwright and novelist named, Samuel Merwin once wrote, *"Every great fortune – every one – is founded on evil, usually on crime."* When discussing corruption in the developing world the famous quote seems to be very relevant. When discussing any nation at any point in history the quote seems to be very relevant. Every government was, at one point or another, simply an organized group of individuals, sometimes even criminals. Whether that group of criminals was the Visigoths invading Rome, or the founding fathers of the United States serving as revolutionaries, at one point they were committing crimes against some already established government and possibly stealing power from another locus of leadership. How we define heroic founding fathers or dishonorable mafias is only in who wins and ultimately writes history.

When any group takes over the leadership of a city, state, or nation then it must have started as an organized group of people. What is the organized leadership of a nation that has the support or fear of the people anyway? The difference between a mafia and a governing body is simply in how we as a people define the two groups. To attain power and acquire recognition from other national governments may be difficult for a group that has just committed a coup d'état, but mafia, revolutionaries, and congress are essentially the same entity with different mandates and constituencies – some legally defined and others illegally operating. To put it another way, under a different set of circumstances the U.S. Congress might be a mafia and the mafia might be congress. Who the mafia is depends on who is writing the laws and who won the argument or war.

Corruption exists in every nation and it is not going anywhere. So, instead of attempting to destroy it one may consider exploiting it – hopefully to destroy it at some point in the future through more natural means. When nations lend to a developing country, often that money never makes it to the intended project. Instead, much of the money is redirected to some corrupt official's western-held, bank account. If the money will not make it to the intended target anyway, then why not pay the official to simply stay out of the way and allow a U.N. agency or U.N. sanctioned NGO power over the remaining funds? Even equipment and resources, such as those used to build roads, are sometimes stolen and sold on the black markets. Paying the official in charge of building the road a livable wage, in other words paying corrupt officials an official salary, might be all that is necessary to avoid a subpar road being built after 30% [75] of the raw materials have been stolen and sold on the black markets. It might even be okay to allow the corrupt officials to assist with the projects if they want – with no possibility of receiving additional funds, of course – but otherwise they would be politely paid to remove all the red tape they may otherwise have created. They would also be expected to protect the project and keep it very close to its original budget, if they remain involved.

Providing corrupt officials the proper incentive to move out of the way indefinitely would require a recurring salary, but it might be less expensive than piecemeal payments to the same officials[19] [76]. Additionally, the recurring payments would reduce transaction costs since the salary would only need to be negotiated one time. There would be no need to renegotiate a bribe every time some action is taken, and if they violate the agreement then they would no longer be paid. Expenses and transaction costs among corrupt officials could be somewhat mitigated by this method, assuming the agreements are enforced. Bribes are really no different than salaries anyway, if they are done the right way; it is only a matter of who is paying and how we define the payments – just like our previous explanation of what defines a mafia or a congress.

Paying the corrupt officials a regular bribe/salary to not intervene in U.N. or NGO projects would help on several fronts. First, the U.N. would be able to directly account for where their money is going. Accountability is a huge problem in the developing world – even the IMF suffers from record keeping deficiencies [58]. Second, they could budget in bribes they are

---

[19] The wage would have to be rather high compared to what they already earn, but given their relative wage when compared to the West, the U.N. salary could still likely be justified.

forced to pay and negotiate to make their spending far more efficient than the current methods. Bribing mid-level managers, for example, could halt theft at the bottom since mid-level managers would have an incentive to properly manage their workers and hold them accountable. Finally, they could ensure the aid is going where they intend. New institutions with improved expectations and accountability can be created, evolving well-defined systems with strong foundations in the communities where our NGOs operate. It may seem like this is a terrible way of developing a nation, and one may even argue that funding corruption is not only unethical but it is most likely inefficient. I do not disagree with either of these arguments, since we are creating a new incentive to be corrupt. However, corruption will naturally disappear in the medium to long-term time frames after proper institutions are adopted [77].

Corruption is not new; in fact we might consider every government official a corrupt individual who is paid by tax dollars, votes for their own raises, and makes laws that directly affect every citizen. I doubt any American would have trouble believing their congress person is corrupted by lobbyists and favors, even if it is not necessarily true. Bribing officials also does not create inefficiencies to the levels that currently already exist outside the institutionalized bribery I am advocating. Corruption can be traced back through many parts of history, but I'll stop at feudalism.

Feudalism was a system in which land and title were granted by a king, queen, or very powerful noble. Common people were not allowed to own land, and could be exiled from their own lands at the whim of the local lord. However, as long as they were in good graces with the local nobility, provided labor and military service as needed, and did not violate the laws of the land, peasants were tentatively granted lands of their own. These lands were not privately held as we would consider them today, could not be turned into assets by the peasant, and they were always subject to change hands if the local lord made some other arrangement. The royals could issue new lands and new titles to anyone they saw fit, and it was always possible for deals to be made whereby some land was taken away from anyone who fell from favor. This form of corrupt government was not defined as corrupt then; it was simply the law of the age. Though it is certainly a terrible system that ensures long-term poverty and a powerful noble class, feudalism lasted, successfully, for roughly 600 years – longer than the Roman Republic which had a far better system of private property and rule of law. Feudalism was very corrupt by our modern measures, yet it was not considered so at the time. It was simply the law. Corruption is defined by the culture and civilization where it exists. There is no problem with our modern definition of corruption, but we can exploit it to favor the most destitute and eventually develop those nations away from corruption, or at least we can minimize its effects.

Mitigation of Corruption

Nobody wants a corrupt government and I hope it has not ruined your day to change the way you view every government employee or representative I am also not in favor of corruption and will be the first to admit that bribing officials is a terrible way of conducting business or governing a nation. To achieve our goal of eliminating poverty, however, it may be necessary to adopt this sort of counter-intuitive policy in the short term. The good thing about a short-term bribing policy is that through our other efforts we will naturally minimize corruption as time progresses.

Private property rights are the very first step toward eliminating world poverty. As discussed before, people must be able to convert their land into capital assets; their creations must be protected, and their innovations must be safe. Without private property rights people have no incentive or ability to break the yoke of poverty. As private property rights are set up we will have to follow the path laid out in the previous section whereby we adopt socialist reforms and convert to capitalism.

While we navigate the fields of development in our U.N. directed nation, good institutions including courts, schools, healthcare, and infrastructure will emerge, and we can begin tapering the salaries we had been providing our corrupt officials. In time we can stop paying lower level officials as new non-corrupt officials are hired, and perhaps reduce payments to more senior representatives as time progresses and tax revenues create salaries where bribes had existed before. Children will be in school, parents will have jobs, infrastructure will be improving, and healthcare will be available to those who need access. The population will observe and grow accustomed to the general level of improvement they are finally experiencing. An improved standard of living will motivate them to continue demanding good governance, and a new era of less corruption will begin to emerge.

Once people know they can defend their rights in courts or to local magistrates, and once they are able to demand better representation, our system of bribing can finally stop entirely. Populations will have a powerful legal system in place, know how to use it to their advantage, and through their improved standard of living, a faith will develop in their newly built economy. Access to banks and the ability to convert land into capital will improve investment, increase employment levels, and will result with increasing economic growth. Health and nutrition will improve since their incomes will be higher and the people will gain access to clean water, sanitation, medicine, and nutrition. Investment into infrastructure will provide access to world markets and communications. Human capital will grow since they will have access to education and healthcare, and capital investment will advance the developing nation into an emerging economy.

As their lives are enhanced they will become accustomed to the higher level of existence; thus, they will demand a more effective and accountable leadership when the U.N. ultimately tapers its programs. The leaders we had been bribing can run for office and become the statesmen the people needed all along, or they can remain corrupt and be removed from their post in future elections. Either way, the system of development through direct intervention and salary-based bribes will come to a natural conclusion.

It may seem counter-intuitive, but development spending will impact everyone around the world. As nations become more self-sufficient, and as people's lives improve, the security of the entire world will be enhanced. Terrorism will decline, suffering will be reduced, and global populations can finally acquire the dignity they deserve and desire. Sometimes I joke that we could end terrorism by making sure everyone in the developing world has air-conditioning, a television and Playstation™, and access to a local McDonald's. This antic truly is not very funny, but there is some truth to the sentiment.

An increased standard of living means increased opportunity costs if people choose to undertake less than desirable actions such as terrorism. International relations can be improved for every nation and all people. Even by intentionally spending some development funds on corruption, subsistence living can be eliminated. It is in the power of our people, wealth, technology, and ability to end world poverty. The world we leave our children and grandchildren will be what we make it. How will our efforts be regarded, with praise and honor or with shame and confusion?

Chapter 8: Conclusion

"We all have our time machines, do not we. Those that take us back are memories... And those that carry us forward are dreams."

– Herbert George Wells

A Journey Through Time

As economies of the world progress into the 21st century, we are likely to see a wildly different landscape than we see today. Free market economies are shifting to more regulatory models while communist nations are aspiring to adopt more free market policies. Ultimately, capitalist nations will never fully adopt socialist policies and communist governments will likely never fully embrace capitalist ideals. However, as every nation wrestles with the various economic philosophies and solutions to their own problems, it is likely in the very distant future everyone will settle very near everyone else, somewhere in the middle of a mixed array of economic models and political policies.

Karl Marx wrote his famous essays *Das Kapital* and *The Communist Manifesto* during the 19th century. When the Gilded Age proved the free market was abusive to labor, governments responded to worker demands after workers of the world ultimately united against many corporations. Purely free markets saw their first regulative actions, and workers saw more rights and higher standards of living than they had retained before. Throughout the 20th century nations fought to reduce or remove poverty within their own borders. Ignoring consequences and without looking to global participation as a viable solution, they sometimes even imposed large tariffs or oppressive quotas. Every nation adopted a policy thought best for its own people and political climate, and no nation's answer was the same as any other. Various economic models were adopted for experimentation and ultimately the capitalist framework has proved to be the most successful so far. As the century progressed freer trade was embraced by many nations, and economies all over the world began enjoying the fruits of growth. Today trade policies have been loosened even more – in fact there is even a free-trade agreement currently being negotiated between the United States and European Union.

Many traditionally free market nations are beginning to adopt more socialistic policies within their borders, with the hope of promoting better health and well-being to their citizens in the 21st century. Previously communist regimes are finally recovering after being shocked into capitalism and they are learning they needed to retain more control than economists had advised – thus they are once again transitioning to more regulation and government intervention. Capitalist nations are attempting to adopt more socialist policies in the presence of several decades of anti-socialist propaganda, and only now are they learning the secondary effects, nuances, and self-imposed difficulties of previous political objections.

If the history of the 20th century teaches us anything it is that old ideas become new and that contemporary ideas fall away only to be revived at a later date when the newest ideas are no longer viable. Adam Smith wrote, *"On the road from the City of Skepticism, I had to pass through the Valley of Ambiguity."* It is certain that nothing is clear except that which is clear at that moment in time. Free markets and socialism both have their place in our world, and both have an environment where they can thrive or fail.

State of the Future of the World

There is a famous thought experiment first discussed by Dr. Erwin Schrodinger about a cat. The cat is placed inside a box with a vile of poison and then the box is sealed closed. At any moment the cat can be thought of as both alive and dead. Unless the box is opened and examined, the state of the cat remains uncertain. I think there is a third option, the cat could have breathed the poison only moments ago and could, therefore, be alive and treatable but on the precipice of death. As such, the cat would deserve a different treatment depending on the state of its existence when the box is finally opened. Attempt to revive the cat if it is dead, treat the cat if it is poisoned, and let the cat run free if it is alive and well.

Markets in the economy are much like Schrodinger's cat; they are nonexistent and nonfunctioning (dead cat), ailing and in need of intervention (sick cat), or efficient and operational (healthy cat). However, until we observe the state of the economy and the status of the operation of the markets, we have not opened the box and cannot possibly make a decision on whether to ignore or intervene in any nation's boom or bust cycle. In the past, economists have identified as free market, Keynesian, or even Marxist; today they often identify as empiricists.

All economic solutions have an environment where they are effective and one where they are not. Just as a doctor should never rule out a treatment on ideological grounds lest the doctor possibly lose a patient after not prescribing the proper medication, we must not rule out any prescription on ideological grounds lest we choose recession or ruin rather than growth and an improved standard of living. If the markets are hardly functioning or perpetuating a state of total malfunction, then centrally plan a way forward and jump start the economy as needed (socialist treatment). If deeper inspection illuminates underlying problems which create pause for concern, then make adjustments and treat the illness before it grows into an incurable cancer (Keynes' treatment). If observation reveals an operational market with few ailments, a good standard of living, and a happy populous, then leave it be (Free market treatment).

I conclude my arguments by stating that no ideology is prudent in every condition of the market; there is a time and place for every idea to thrive and also for those same ideas to fail. On a continuum of absolutes made popular by television and radio personalities, every possibility is potentially right and wrong, but entrenched ideologies corner policy makers and limit their possibilities. Every state of the economy contains a unique set of circumstances that requires a unique set of actions. Adopting a single ubiquitous approach based on any specific ideal is disastrous to our economy, destructive to our world and ruinous to all humankind. Ignoring any particular approach because of one's ideals can have the same calamitous affect.

The World We Leave Behind

The current state of the world is simple disarray. States fight for control because of fear, ideology, religion, resources, and trade. Warlords and terrorists fight over manpower, wealth, political clout, ideals, and prestige. Politicians wage a war of words through elections, issuing real solutions or false promises, the status quo or grandiose ideas, and ultimately become leaders or lemmings. The media chooses sides, reports both truth and lies, spreads both knowledge and rumors, and voices both unforgiving and unqualified speculation. The people of the world continue to suffer as they fight to put food on their table and keep their families healthy. The confusion produced either through the intentional or careless televising of misinformation, coupled with the incentive to gather ever higher ratings, produce nothing of value and only serves to harm the public welfare. Unfortunately, the future is uncertain and the way forward remains, as always, unclear.

The world we leave behind for our children and grand-children should certainly be one forged by an open-minded leadership. Closing ourselves to particular ideologies because of decades of propaganda, because of a lack of understanding, or because of a cornucopia of misunderstanding, is not how we will ensure a higher standard of living for all of earth's inhabitants. Accepting all ideas in a world of possibility and ruling out nothing because of preconceived notions is essential to our success. Entertaining all ideas as possibly viable and allowing no idea to go unheard is how we will improve our world for future generations. Whether we accept socialism or capitalism or some combination of the two should be a product of our culture and the condition of the markets, not of our politics and propaganda.

I will close this book with a few things I believe are certain. Economies of the world will grow and shrink as nations – acting in their own self-interest – adopt policies to best fit their existing market conditions, which in turn will affect other nations' markets and circumstances. Politics will unfortunately impede progress by disallowing the best solutions offered when those solutions are politically unpopular and thus progress will be slowed. I believe it is important, whether we hope to protect resources, promote democracy, or halt oppression, to accept that every solution has its place in our world and that only market conditions should dictate when particular policies are adopted or when they are ignored.

Sometimes the way forward is not through the most efficient economic model, but first through some inefficient allocations of resources to set the stage for a more efficient future outcome. Effective policies do not depend on good or evil intentions, but on the culture and markets where they are adopted. In the words of George Washington, "*Government is not reason; it is not eloquent; it is force. Like fire, it is a dangerous servant and a fearful master.*" Open markets, open forums, open dialogue, and open minds are all that is required for a strong people to achieve an increased standard of living for everyone on earth.

Although economics is dismal and political science is sometimes obstructive and antithetical to global economic growth, I remain hopeful for our future and our world. Progress is not made by those who staunchly entrench themselves in the realm of old ideals and fearful of change; it is made by those who blaze forth against all odds and sometimes in direct opposition to the common knowledge of the day. Those who achieve progress do not accept axioms, they create them. We must create a new paradigm before we can defeat world poverty and promote greater standards of living for all. We must learn that economic models cannot be based on pure capitalism or pure socialism; they must fit a constantly shifting continuum of ideas where sometimes the answer is a seemingly undesirable amalgamation of conflicting wisdom. I am an empiricist, I prefer free market solutions, and I believe in Adam Smith's *Invisible Hand*. Sometimes conditions dictate different solutions, however, and that is why I called this book, "*Three-handed Economist.*" I started this book with a quote from John F. Kennedy, and now I'll end with an equally inspiring quote from the same, "*No problem or human destiny is beyond human beings. Man's reason and spirit have often solved the seemingly unsolvable, and we believe they can do it again.*"

Works Cited

[1]   R. F. Bruner and S. D. Carr, The Panic of 1907, Hoboken: John Wiley & Sons, Inc., 2007.

[2]   J. Sachs, The End of Poverty, New York: Penguin Group, 2005.

[3]   M. Josephson, The Robber Barons: The Great American Capitalists, New Brunswick: Transaction Publishers, 2011.

[4]   G. M. Walton and H. Rockoff, History of the American Economy, Mason: South-Western Cengage Learning, 2010.

[5]   J. W. Davidson, B. Delay, C. L. Heyrman, M. H. Lytle and M. B. Stoff, Nation of Nations, New York: McGraw Hill Companies, Inc., 2008.

[6]   R. Rabin, "Warnings unheeded: a history of child lead poisoning," *American Journal of Public Health,* vol. 79, no. 12, pp. 1668-1674, 1989.

[7]   D. McKenzie, "CNN.com," CNN, 29 May 2013. [Online]. Available: http://www.cnn.com/2013/05/28/world/asia/china-cancer-villages-mckenzie. [Accessed 30 July 2013].

[8]   K. Bradsher, "China Begins Inquiry Into Tainted Baby Formula," *The New York Times,* p. A10, 13 September 2008.

[9]   "United States Department of Agriculture," August 2005. [Online]. Available: http://www.fsis.usda.gov/OPPDE/larc/Policies/Labeling_Poli cy_Book_082005.pdf. [Accessed 30 June 2014].

[10] P. Xizhe, "Demographic Consequences of the Great Leap Forward in China's Provinces," *Population and Development Review,* vol. 4, no. 13, pp. 639-70, 1987.

[11] E. S. Steinfeld, Forging Reform in China, New York: Cambridge University Press, 1998.

[12] M. Friedman, Capitalism and Freedom, Chicago: The University of Chicago Press, 2002.

[13] A. Del Mar, A History of Precious Metals From the Earliest Times to the Present, New York: Cambridge Encyclopedia Company, 2005.

[14] L. Mises, Human Action, Auburn: The Ludwig von Mises Institute, 1998.

[15] G. P. Shultz and K. W. Dam, Economic Policy Beyond the Headlines, 2nd ed., Chicago: University of Chicago Press, 1998.

[16] "Bank of England," United Kingdom, [Online]. Available: http://www.bankofengland.co.uk/education/Pages/inflation/ti meline/chart.aspx. [Accessed 6 June 2013].

[17] J. Goodwin, Lords of the Horizons, New York: Picador, 1998.

[18] D. E. French, Early Speculative Bubbles, Auburn: The Ludwig von Mises Institute, 2009.

[19] M. Thornton and R. B. Ekelund, Tariffs, Blockades, and Inflation: The Economics of the Civil War, Wilmington: Scholarly Resources Inc., 2004.

[20] M. Thornton and R. B. J. Ekelund, Tariffs, Blockades, and Inflation: The Economics of the Civil War, Wilmington: Scholarly Resources Inc., 2004.

[21] G. E. Griffin, The Creature from Jekyll Island: A Second Look at the Federal Reserve, Westlake Village: American Media, 2002.

[22] T. Todd, The Balance of Power, Kansas City: Public Affairs Department of the Federal Reserve Bank of Kansas City, 2009.

[23] J. D. Gwartney, R. L. Stroup, R. S. Sobel and D. A. Macpherson, Economics: Private and Public Choice, Mason: Sout-Western Cengage Learning, 2009.

[24] A. Fergusson, When Money Dies, New York: William Kimber and Co. Ltd., 1975.

[25] A. Nove, An Economic History of the USSR: 1917-1991, 3rd ed., New York: Penguin Group, 1993.

[26] M. Rothbard, America's Great Depression, Kansas City: Sheed and Ward, Inc., 1975.

[27] "U.S. Mint," [Online]. Available: http://www.usmint.gov/about_the_mint/index.cfm?action=Pr oductionFigures. [Accessed 18 December 2013].

[28] B. Pisani, "The Billion Dollar Business of Diamonds, From Mining to Retail," CNBC, 2012.

[29] "National Health Expenditure Accounts," [Online]. Available: http://www.cms.gov/Research-Statistics-Data-and-

Systems/Statistics-Trends-and-
Reports/NationalHealthExpendData/NationalHealthAccounts
Historical.html. [Accessed 16 May 2014].

[30] R. A. Stevens, "Health Care in the Early 1960s," *Healthcare Financing Review,* vol. 18, no. 2, pp. 11-22, 1996.

[31] "Income, Poverty, and Health Insurance Coverage in the United States: 2012," [Online]. Available: http://www.census.gov/prod/2013pubs/p60-245. [Accessed 16 May 2014].

[32] "OECD Health Statistics 2013 - Frequently Requested Data".

[33] P. S. Hussey, G. F. Anderson, R. Osborn, C. Feek, V. McLaughlin, J. Millar and A. Epstein, "How Does Quality of Care Compare In Five Countries," *Health Affairs,* vol. 23, no. 3, pp. 89-99, 2004.

[34] A. Tandon, C. J. Murray, J. A. Lauer, D. B. Evans and , "Measuring Overall Health System Performance For 191 Countries," *World Health Organization,* no. Discussion Paper Series, 30.

[35] L. Siciliani, M. Borowitz and V. Moran, "Waiting Time Policies in the Health Sector: What Works? OECD Health Policy Studies," *OECD Publishing,* 2013.

[36] R. Reich, "Raising Taxes on Corporations that Pay Their CEOs Royally and Treat Their Workers Like Serfs," 21 April 2014. [Online]. Available: http://robertreich.org/post/83456610643. [Accessed 16 June 2014].

[37] X. Gabaix and A. Landier, "Why has CEO Pay Increased So Much?," *The Quarterly Journal of Economics,* vol. 123, no. 1, pp. 49-100, 2008.

[38] "Department of Health and Human Services," 2013. [Online]. Available: http://aspe.hhs.gov/poverty/13poverty.cfm. [Accessed 19 December 2013].

[39] "Amnesty International," [Online]. Available: http://www.amnestyusa.org/our-work/countries/asia-and-the-pacific/china. [Accessed 28 February 2014].

[40] "China Labor Watch," 2014. [Online]. Available: https://www.chinalaborwatch.org. [Accessed 31 May 2014].

[41] A. O. Ebenstein, W. Ebenstein and E. Fogelman, Today's

Isms, Englewood Cliffs: Prentice Hall, 1994.

[42] A. Nove, An Economid History of the USSR, New York: Penguin, 1993.

[43] J. Krejc, Social structure in divided Germany, London: Croom Helm, 1976.

[44] J. G. Zivin and M. Neidell, "The Impact of Pollution on Worker Productivity," *American Economic Review,* vol. 102, no. 2, pp. 3652-73, 2012.

[45] G. Glomm and B. Ravidumar, "Public versus Private Investment in Human Capital Endogenous Growth and Income Inequality," *Journal of Political Economy,* vol. 4, pp. 818-34, 1992.

[46] J. B. Knight and R. H. Sabot, "Educational Policy and Labour Productivity: An Output Accounting Exercise," *The Economic Journal,* vol. 97, no. 385, pp. 199-214, 1987.

[47] E. Duflo, "Schooling and Labor Market Consequences of School Construction in Indonesia: Evidence from an Unusual Policy Experiment," *The American Economic Review,* vol. 91, no. 4, pp. 795-813, 2001.

[48] B. S. Gates and M. A. Mackin, Showing Up for Life: Thoughts on the Gifts of a Lifetime, New York: Broadway Books, 2009.

[49] S. Arora, "Health, Human Productivity, and Long-Term Economic Growth," *The Journal of Economic History,* vol. 61, no. 3, pp. 699-749, 2001.

[50] R. H. Coase, "The Lighthouse in Economics," *Journal of Law and Economics,* vol. 17, no. 2, pp. 357-76, 1974.

[51] "World Bank," 2014. [Online]. Available: http://data.worldbank.org/news/40prct-wrld-pop-dont-use-imprvd-sanitation. [Accessed 28 February 2014].

[52] A. Banerjee and E. Duflo, Poor Economics, New York: Public Affairs, 2011.

[53] W. Hinton, Fanshen, New York: Monthly Review Press, 2008.

[54] F. Dikotter, Mao's Great Famine, Edinburgh: Worldcolor Fairfield, 2010.

[55] R. Ffrench-Davis, Economic Reforms in Chile: From Dictatorship to Democracy, London: Saffron House, 2010.

[56] R. Ffrench-Davis, Economic Reforms in Chile: From Dictatorship to Democracy, New York: Palgrave Macmillan, 2002.

[57] A. Martinek, "Hello Czech Republic," 1 January 2010. [Online]. Available: http://www.czech.cz/en/Discover-CZ/Facts-about-the-Czech-Republic/History/The-History-of-the-Czech-Economy. [Accessed 4 April 2014].

[58] W. Easterly, White Man's Burden: Why the West's Efforts to Aid the Rest Have Done So Much Ill and So Little Good, London: Penguin Press, 2006.

[59] "The World Bank," 2014. [Online]. Available: http://data.worldbank.org/country/czech-republic. [Accessed 10 June 2014].

[60] D. Yergin and J. Stanislaw, The Commanding Heights, New York: Simon and Schuster, 2002.

[61] J. Denman and P. McDonald, "Unemployment statistics from 1881 to the present day," *Labor Market Trends,* no. Special Feature.

[62] "HM Revenue & Customs," [Online]. Available: http://www.hmrc.gov.uk/rates/. [Accessed 21 May 2014].

[63] D. Acemoglu and J. Robinson, Why Nations Fail, New York: Crown Publishing Group, 2012.

[64] S. L. Engerman and K. L. Sokoloff, "Colonialism, Inequality, and Long-Run Paths of Development," *National Bureau of Economic Research, Working Paper Series,* no. 11057, 2005.

[65] H. De Soto, The Mystery of Capital: Why Capitalism Triumphs in the West and Fails Everywhere Else, New York: Basic Books, 2000.

[66] D. Moyo, Dead Aid: Why Aid is not Working and How There is a Better Way for Africa, New York: Farrar, Straus and Giroux, 2009.

[67] P. Collier, The Bottom Billion: Why the Poorest Countries Are Failing, and What Can Be Done About It, New York: Oxford University Press Inc., 2007.

[68] "Global Report: UNAIDS report on the global AIDS epidemic 2013," Joint United Nations Programme on HIV/AIDS (UNAIDS), 2013.

[69] M. Tupy, "The Breadbasket is Still a Basket Case," *Foreign*

Policy, 25 July 2013.

[70] "From Breadbasket to basket case," *The Economist,* 27 June 2002.

[71] "Progress on Sanitation and Drinking-Water: 2010 Update," World Health Organization and UNICEF, 2010.

[72] "The Water Project," [Online]. Available: http://thewaterproject.org/poverty. [Accessed 12 June 2014].

[73] W. Duggan, Napoleon's Glance, New York: Thunder's Mouth Press/Nation Books, 2002.

[74] "United Nations Development Programme," [Online]. Available: http://open.undp.org. [Accessed 9 April 2014].

[75] V. Alexeeva, G. Padam and C. Queiroz, "Monitoring Road Works Contracts and Unit Costs for Enhanced Governance in Sub-Saharan Africa," World Bank, Washington D.C., 2008.

[76] C. V. Rijckeghem and B. Weder, "Bureaucratic corruption and the rate of temptation: do wages in the civil service affect corruption, and by how much?," *Journal of Development Economics,* vol. 65, no. 2, pp. 307-331, 2001.

[77] V. F. Misangyi, G. R. Weaver and H. Elms, "Ending Corruption: The Interplay Among Institutional Logics, Resources, and Institutional Entrepreneurs," *Academy of Management Review,* vol. 39, no. 3, pp. 750-770, 2008.

Further Suggested Reading

1. Hayek, F. A. (1944) *The Road to Serfdom.* London, EN: George Routledge & Sons

2. Keynes, J. M., (1965) *The General Theory of Employment, Interest, and Money.* Orlando, FL: First Harvest/Harcourt, Inc.

3. Mises, L. (2009) *The Theory of Money and Credit.* Auburn, AL: Ludwig von Mises Institute

4. Mises, L. (1962) *Socialism: An Economic and Sociological Analysis*. New Haven, CT: Yale University Press
5. Marx, K., & Engels, F. (2012) *Das Kapital*. New York, NY: Aristeus Books
6. Yunus, M. (2007) *Banker to the Poor: Micro-Lending and the Battle Against World Poverty*. New York, NY: Public Affairs
7. Rawls, J. (2001) *Justice as Fairness*. Cambridge, MA: The Belknap Press of Harvard University Press
8. Diamond, J. (2005) *Guns, Germs, and Steel: The Fates of Human Societies*. New York, NY: W.W. Norton and Company
9. Coggan, P. (2012) *Paper Promises*. New York, NY: Penguin Group
10. Hubbard, G. R., & Duggan W. (2009) *The Aid Trap*. New York, NY: Columbia University Press
11. McKinnon, R. (2013) *The Unloved Dollar Standard: From Bretton Woods to the Rise of China*. New York, NY: Oxford University Press
12. Ariely, D. (2008) *Predictably Irrational*. New York, NY: Harper Collins
13. Biggs, B. (2008) *Wealth, War, and Wisdom*. Hoboken, NJ: John Wiley and Sons, Inc.
14. Friedman, M., & Friedman, R. (1979) *Free to Choose*. San Diego, CA: Harcourt Brace and Company
15. Alpert, D. (2013) *The Age of Oversupply: Overcoming the Greatest Challenge to the Global Economy*. New York, NY: Penguin Group
16. Holland, J. (2010) *Fifteen Biggest Lies About the Economy: and Everything Else the Right Does not Want You to Know About Taxes, Jobs, and Corporate America*. Hoboken, NJ: John Wiley & Sons, Inc.
17. Bastiat, F. (2007) *The Law*. Auburn, AL: SoHo Books

18. Gladwell, M. (2005) *blink*. New York, NY: Little, Brown, and Company

19. Fromkin, D. (1989) *A Peace to End All Peace*. New York, NY: Henry Holt and Company

20. Hansen, A. (1953) *A Guide to Keynes*. New York, NY: McGraw Hill Book Company, Inc.

21. Palmer, A. (1992) *Decline and Fall of the Ottoman Empire*. New York, NY: Barnes and Noble Books

22. Stent, G. (1978) *Paradoxes of Progress*. San Francisco, CA: W. H. Freeman and Company

23. Lach, S., & Schanckerman, M. (2003). Incentives and Invention in Universities. *National Bureau of Economic Research*, Retrieved May 25th, 2013, from http://www.nber.org/CRIW/papers/lach.pdf

24. Nunn, N. (2006). The Long-Term Effects of Africa's Slave Trades. Quarterly Journal of Economics, 123 (1): 139-176.

25. Miller, D. (1977). Socialism and the Market. Political Theory, 5(4): 473-490.

26. Kramer, M. (2010) "Stalin, Soviet Policy, and the Consolidation of a Communist Bloc in Eastern Europe, 1944-53." In *Stalinism Revisited: The Establishment of Communist Regimes in East-Central Europe*, edited by Vladimir Tismaneanu, 51-102. Budapest; New York: Central European University Press, 2010.